MANIPULATION PSYCHOLOGY

Learn Quickly The Secrets of Manipulation Techniques, Hypnosis, Body Language and Mind Control

by Dylan Black

3

due to the information herein, either directly or indirectly. The author owns all copyrights not held by the publisher.

The information herein is provided for educational purpose exclusively and is universal. The presentation of the data is without contractual agreement or any kind of warranty assurance.

All trademarks inside this book are for clarifying purposes only and are possessed by the owners themselves, not allied with this document.

Disclaimer

All erudition supplied in this book are specified for educational and academic purpose only. The author is not in any way in charge for any outcomes that emerge from using this book. Constructive efforts have been made to render information that is both precise and effective, however the author is not to be held answerable for the accuracy or use/misuse of this information.

Foreword

I will like to thank you for taking the very first step of trusting me and deciding to purchase/read this life-transforming book. Thanks for investing your time and resources on this product.

I can assure you of precise outcomes if you will diligently follow the specific blueprint I lay bare in the information handbook you are currently checking out. It has transformed lives, and I strongly believe it will equally transform your own life too.

All the information I provided in this *Do It Yourself* piece is easy to absorb and practice.

Table of Contents

INTRODUCTION 9

CHAPTER ONE 11

Codes of Influence 11

The Charm Code 11

The Secret Handshake Code 29

CHAPTER TWO 47

Manipulation 47

Lying 59

Omission lying 60

Denial 60

Justification 61

Strategies of Manipulation 66

CHAPTER THREE 79

Mind Control 79

CHAPTER FOUR 85

Hypnosis 85

CHAPTER FIVE 119

Persuasion 119

CHAPTER SIX 123

Deception 123

CHAPTER SEVEN   125

   Body Language Codes   125

CHAPTER EIGHT   149

   Setting Boundary Not To Be Manipulated   149

INTRODUCTION

It takes place too often. People who are struggling with low self-esteem end up getting stuck in a relationship where they're being manipulated by their loved one or perhaps a child. They're the unwitting targets of individuals who experience emotional disorders or psychological conditions that move them to act in a manipulative way.

The result of this manipulation can be unpleasant for the victims, but specifically for the manipulators themselves, as they have a hard time to maintain relationships with loved ones or colleagues. Manipulators can end up separating themselves in their attempts to manage a circumstance and feed their need for power to build themselves up. These isolated people might find it difficult to break the cycle, hence discovering that it tends to feed itself.

Overtime, victims might become sensitive to the manipulation and end the relationships altogether. A manipulator can also discover that they will control themselves into believing their actions are needed for the wellness of themselves or the individual whom they are manipulating.

9

Manipulators have a few primary inspirations that may be shocking to those being preyed on:

- Must advance their purpose and individual benefit at the expense of others.
- Are power starving and need to feel exceptional in a relationship.
- If they are the dominant one in a relationship at all times, are control freaks and require to feel as.
- Have low self-esteem and needs to have power over another to raise their perception of themselves.
- See manipulation as merely a game due to a psychopathic propensity.

If you find that you understand somebody like this, be aware of their actions and yours. Check out to find out the features of a manipulator, and how to deal with one in your relationship.

CHAPTER ONE

Codes of Influence

The Charm Code and Special Attractiveness

Many studies have discussed the external appearance of man and its effect on his life and others. A lot of these studies have revealed with no doubt that the person who has a gorgeous or charming external look is to be more appreciated than others. Likewise, these studies have shown that humans as a whole think about and value the outer look.

One research study in the United States among the major universities showed that the female students who are considered lovely receive higher grades more than those who are not considered to be gorgeous or more than their male student colleagues. The speakers who are good-looking and captivating are more persuasive and helpful to their students compared to non-handsome. Attractive ladies are more able and persuading to change the views of male customers in particular, compared to the influence of others who are seen as just regular in their external appearance.

Another study has revealed that workers in restaurants who have an excellent looking appearance get things more than others with a natural look!

But when did this start, and how did we get to this level?

A new study offered some examples of a group of children. It has shown that children took more time looking surprisingly at the images of the most upper class compared to others. You will be amazed at the vast quantity of these studies and researches in many fields. That indeed shows that we as humans enjoy being around people with attractive external appearance, as we consider them smarter, healthier, more reliable, more interesting, enthusiastic, and wealthier than others.

Is this true? Isn't this trivial? Does this mean if I do not look gorgeous, I should be considered, silly, weak, and dull person? The answer is both yes and no!

No, because the lower class individuals are not necessarily less attractive, and at the very same time, the charming people are not always the smartest, the most powerful, and the healthiest!

And yes, because this is what the human being's mind is assessing. If the external appearance is terrible, the person will never get much adoration from others, and definitely, this has nothing to do if you were born with a good looking face or not!

External Appearance and paying attention is absurd! Thousands of wisdom pieces and sayings, which are all real, and no doubt about their reliability talked about this principle.

However, we need not reject the fact that we love to be with appealing people more than being with others who are less attractive, and there is no doubt about this too! Therefore, we need to go back to the definition of the appealing external look; it is not only the great looking face, is not the gorgeous body. Not only those blown lips, not merely the big female breast, not just the blonde hair, not just those green eyes, and indeed it is not just that expensive match! It's all of these together!

The significant aspect of this subject is that this information remains in your hands, and you can completely alter them or add them to the external look whenever you desire. They are at your disposal and discretion, and if you do not have a great looking face, this is not a problem! It does not matter! You have the secret methods that we are going to learn now, as those techniques understand how the mind thinks and determines if you are beautiful or not. Without these secret methods, you are in real trouble.

The Mind of others is set to accept attractive individuals in their appearance more than others, so stop lamenting! You know that you are the most recognized and stunning person, but we will add the appealing external appearance, why? Because within only four seconds, and before you utter any word, others will determine if they like you or not.

Therefore, an appealing external look is a ticket for the initial acceptance of any other person. Let us get it now! And keep in mind that the attractive external look is the most crucial drive for high self-esteem, so we need to get it now!

Clothes (Men and Women)

To be considered attractive, you will continuously be in the best suitable clothes for you; you have to be moderate in your style to choose your clothing, do not go too far beyond the average. Brightly-colored clothes are inappropriate, and apparel with unique styles is not acceptable; stay within the appropriate level!! If you like different things, you need to stop it now.

You have to be within the socially essential limitations, and this is not restrictive for your liberty. But you do not use clothing just for you; instead, you wear to look better in the eyes of others as the famous saying goes: "(Eat what you like, and use and dress what others like)!"

"You have to be always 10% much better than those around you."

If you are going to a meeting and understand that all coming to the meeting are going to wear suits, but no tie, you will wear a match with a tie. If you are going to meet friends at the café, and you know that everyone would wear jeans with T-shirts, you would wear jeans with a shirt more detailed to be formal, and so on! You are 10 percent better than those around you.

Do not go to a meeting where you know that the client is going to wear jeans, for example. And you go there with a tie. Why? As humans, we like people who appear like us in everything. You will add 10%, specifically for particular attractiveness, and to be at a higher level than the others; to be in the Alpha State! This applies entirely to both ladies and males.

For Men

Stay away from clothing with exotic design and colors, always remain in the average.

-Wear clothes with similar colors, and if you do not know how to do it when you buy, ask one of the ladies around you if the colors match, given that women are masters in matching colors!

Ties must match with quiet colors and styles. Stay away from ties loaded with colors, as they reflect lousy taste!

Do not wear loose clothing or extremely tight clothing; your dress must fit your body snugly.

For Women

As mentioned above for men.

In addition to that, do not use scandalous clothing revealing your body. Research has shown that women are wearing outrageous clothes exposing their bodies, such as miniskirts. These tight or open clothes show their bodies, they get more extended interviews but less convincing to the other party. Yes, I, as a man, I like to take as much time as possible sitting down with a female wearing seductive clothing, but I will never take her seriously, why? Because my mind will respond to the essential question: Why does this female dress like that? One of the most common answers is that she does not have self-esteem, so she wants to expose her body for more external approval; she is readily available at low-cost.

She is beautiful, but she reveals her body scandalously! In other words, she is calling your unconscious simply to look at her body and see if you need any part of it. Many ladies neither know, nor confess that this is the reason. In reality, they don't know because this is what is happening inside them. All they are looking for is to look attractive.

Research in Western Europe and America has shown that a woman considered attractive wears more decent clothes! Another study has shown that the more you cover your body, the more affection of the other person you will get. Try it now, the way of talking will differ, especially at work. The focus will be more on ideas and products or anything you are trying to convince others of. Try it now! Use outrageous revealing clothing and go to a meeting, or to meet somebody, and attempt to talk in an important subject—your opinion in the policy of a specific country or suggestions to a theory of physics. You will find out that the acceptance and focus of others on the subject is becoming less; instead, you will find that most of them will never take your words seriously. Yes, they will entirely concur with your opinion and smile. Still, they will attempt to leave the base on other subjects to develop a special relationship, dating, or something closer to sex, why?

Easy! It is as if we are showing a sex film in front of someone, and ask him to enjoy the sex film. At the same time, we start discussing the space in the ozone layer and its various environmental impacts. Can you picture how the discussion would be?

Now, the next time, wear better cloth and try to cover as much as you can of your body and go to the same meeting. When you start the conversation, you will be shocked by the style of communication in general. You will be astonished by the quality of admiration you are going to get. This is remarkable, isn't it? Persuasion experts are individuals in the **Alpha State**. Because you are in alpha state, your body belongs to you and is not for a program.

For that reason, using your body in persuasion methods and processes will not work. It holds that the client might purchase from you but, he will take a piece of your body, and thus you lost. You have the offer, but you have lost their trust and appreciation for you. Therefore, you need to wear the right clothes fit for the meeting, with as much modesty as possible.

The Wedding Ring

Women

If you are using a large and attractive wedding ring and you are going to meet another woman, take it off immediately because it will fire up some feelings of jealousy for women. We need to avoid this during the persuasion process. You always need to wear a smooth ring in any persuasion you are about to execute.

Men

Use a comfortable ring if you are married, to be of silver, considering that using a gold ring will give a sign of a man's softness and weakness in the mind of others, so always keep away from gold!

Nails

Ladies

If your nails are more than 1/2 inch long, cut and clip them immediately. Long nails are a terrible sign of deep space in your life.

Stay away from colored nails with exceptional colors, especially intense red since it is the color primarily used by prostitutes, and definitely, you are not one of them. Stay away from this color when you go out to meet other individuals or in a company meeting.

Always go to a store or beauty shop to trim and clean your nails.

Men

You should trim your nails frequently.

Your nails must always be clean and trimmed in an acceptable pattern.

"Persuasion experts always have appealing and clean hands!"

Glasses

You need to keep away from wearing glasses as much as possible because they can minimize your beauty instantly and place a barrier between you and the others. People are more comfortable when they can see the eyes of the other party. Try to sit down with a good friend while wearing sunglasses and start talking to him, and you will discover that he becomes upset, and he will often ask you to take off your glasses! The glasses are a real barrier between people, so if you can wear contact lenses, it is better, or if you need to perform vision correction at a healthcare facility, do it as it is readily available in almost every healthcare facility. Attempt to use smaller sized glasses without the frames if you are not able to do it! You can wear any type of sunglasses, but do not use them when you are inside any location like some individuals often do. Stay away from blind imitations.

Hair

For a man, it certainly varies from one culture to another, but generally speaking, try to keep facial hair and moustaches regularly clean. For women, you need to take care of this too, some women have fluff above the upper lip, you have to remove it, and there are many ways to do that.

Keeping hair in the nose and ear is undesirable. Get rid of it right away since it gives a feeling of disgust to others and the absence of hygiene.

Head hair should always be short and clean for men as long hair that reaches the neck can mean that others may never take a person seriously. You have to choose between being an expert in persuasion, or to keep your hair long. If you suffer from an absence of hair or balding, have your haircut or trimmed instantly. A person who keeps some hair to cover balding has a week character and has no self-confidence. For that reason, have a full haircut if you are experiencing baldness. For women, you continuously have to keep up on your hair. Keep away from having long hair, given that this is an indication that you spend a lot of time at home on taking care of your hair only. Stay away from dying your hair with weird colors that are unsuitable for your face and your skin color. If you are with a full look and closer to be round, try to make your hair longer and let it cover both sides of your face. This should be at your discretion and your hairdresser's disposal to choose the best hairstyle.

Fashion, Jewellery, and Accessories

For men, you need to stay away from fashion jewelry other than your wedding ring, watch, or engagement ring. Earrings or wearing pendants are strictly prohibited!

For women, you can wear small earrings that do not draw much attention! Stay away from huge or glossy size precious jewelry because you are not in a jewelry show. You are working in a long-term process of convincing others; therefore, you can use what you desire of jewelry, so long as it is simple.

Hygiene

You need to be clean continually and to smell of cleanliness. Have your shower or bath at least once a day. Use deodorants as much as possible, but keep away from exhibiting scent deodorants. Purchase one without fragrance; it is better!

Perfumes

The usage of fragrances is essential to an unexpected level. Because of your smell, you might lose a relevant contract, or you may get approval. The use of perfume is considered an art in itself. We do not have adequate time here to describe it. However, we will focus on some essential points:

In work interviews or meetings with people you do not know, avoid the use of perfume; instead, try to keep yourself clean with natural smell without using perfume. You do not know if your client likes your smell or if he might be averse to such smell. For that reason, it does not worth losing the contract simply because of your perfume. Try to keep yourself clean, and if you need to use perfume, use the light ones!

In casual meetings, the choice of perfume differs depending on the environment and the nature of the meeting. In the summertime, stay away entirely from perfumes with a strong smell, whereas, in the winter season, you can do that, as it will reflect some warmth in the mind of others. For women, using perfumes with unusual smell may decrease others' regard for you since it is an indicator stating loudly to others: "Please! I'm here, look at me." You should have a uniquely warm and mild scent to be smelled just by those around you, but not everybody in the street, so be mindful!

Teeth and Mouth

Teeth should be clean and neat, and if not so, go to the dentist and fix them as much as possible, especially if you have yellow-colored teeth. You need to maintain your teeth because of the value of an attractive smile to be shown on your external appearance. For the mouth, it should always smell good. If you smoke, you ought to use mint chewing gum always after cigarette smoking.

Cosmetics (Makeup)

Using a lot of cosmetics will decrease the level of others' consideration of your views regardless of what that view is. You are attractive without makeup. Putting a lot of cosmetics will make your face shout stating: "You all, look at me, I know that my face is ugly, but thanks to this gorgeous make-up that makes me look attractive because I do not trust my appearance without them." So, the less you use these cosmetics, the much better you will look. Be close to your natural self, use as much as you want of cosmetics, but make sure to use beautiful and light colors, and do not ever turn your face to be like one painting of Picasso!

Body

The body is you; it is what others see at the start before they understand your terrific and unusual inner value! Your body needs to be always excellent, stay away from getting extremely thin (If you are not suffering from a particular illness). Being lightweight for reasons aside from a disease is proof of your personality weak point and will reduce your confidence. Stay away from weight difficulties, it is stark evidence of your failure to manage yourself. A healthy person controls himself and his food intake. All of us need to exercise daily, do not say I don't have time. Without having a lovely body, you will get nothing. You will lose your confidence.

I am not saying you need to be an expert in bodybuilding. On the contrary, many people do not like the body filled with big muscles, but you have to be fit. The most important thing is to get rid of your belly fat. There are many kinds of exercise you can engage in to lower your belly. Do not get deceived by the easy manner in which everyone is marketing herbs, magic recipes, and silly devices; ideal exercise along with an appropriate diet should be the focus!

Exercise will increase your blood circulation, leading to more food for your mind and all your body systems. This will lead to more positive energy and strength. It is an essential aspect of the persuasion process as you will not be able to become an expert in persuasion without exercising everyday, even for only 10 minutes a day! Start now!

Bags You Carry

For men: It needs to be of a small size as much as possible if you need to carry a bag. Therefore, any bag containing more than a laptop is not appropriate at all! For ladies! If you are going to an organization meeting, carry a small purse as much as possible too, a bag that can just accommodate your money and some private stuff. Big bags can indicate that you are an unorganized person, and the client is going to recognize that they will suffer dealing with you because you are disorganized in your work.

Big bags containing thousands of things stay in your home or the car exterior.

For that reason, when we discussed the external appeal or attractive look, we did not mean that you ought to look like Brad Pitt to become a specialist in persuasion. The external appeal of attractive appearance means all those things that we have discussed, which are considered the special attraction laws that you have, so as the mind of others will say," this individual is attractive".

Therefore, these are a few small details; however, they are as important as you can envision in offering instant external beauty. Forget Hollywood and those publications that declare that you have to have a big chest (breast), slim nose, and bid blown lips; you are not a showgirl. Instead, you are an expert in persuasion and human control. You are attractive in the way that the mind acknowledges. Avoid feeling that you are not appropriately lovely always, and you have to use this cream and that emollient or moisturizer to become more attractive and more appropriate. This is wrong, and you know it. You are a super person, and you will always be so. Therefore you need to act and behave as an ALPHA individual.

The Secret Handshake Code

Shaking hands began amongst people since the beginning of humankind, where people used to raise their hands as a sign of not carrying weapons in their hands. This process has developed through the ages, to be a manner we handle each other every day in our lives. When we meet somebody, we shake hands with him as a sign of regard at the beginning or the end of the meeting. When we meet another person; we get to shake hands with him, the unusual thing about it is that we in our youth, have learned that there is a kind code in all of us; If someone extends his hand to shake yours, you got to reciprocate. You will be much stunned about the value of such a relocation (handshaking) in the persuasion process, or even more than that, and you will learn how you are going to enforce your control entirely from the start by a handshake only. However, before we get even more into the methods and codes, let us learn more about the practices of handshaking and their meanings in the mind, who is the dominant individual? Who is the better person?

There are three primary forms of handshaking:

1. Dominant

2. Managed

3. Equal

Dominant

With this handshake, you declare that you remain in control and you are alpha individual in the mind of the other person. As in the picture below, your palm is down.

Through this handshake, you immediately declare that you will be in control of the meeting from now on, and the mind of the other party will recognize it instantly. It is through this handshake that you are forcing the other person to shake your hands as he is a beta person.

Managed

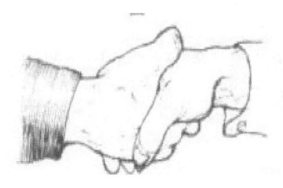

It is such that you will shake the other person as displayed in the picture, where the palm is upwards. Where you are quickly saying to the other person that you are manageable and you are a beta person.

Equality

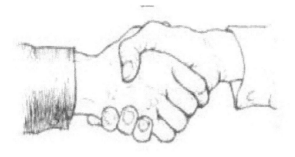

It is just the equality between the parties in force and control, as in the image listed above. The mind will instantly understand that you both are in authority, and it will look for more clues by talking between you as to determine who is the dominant one.

Now, we learn more about a few of the kinds of handshakes that are repeated frequently between individuals, learn about their significances in the mind, and develop techniques to use these forms.

Hand Hug (Double Hander)

This method is most frequently used by political leaders where the individual is trying to validate to the other party that he is truthful and trustworthy. Still, you have to beware when using this technique with somebody whom you do not know, as it will make his mind doubt the reason for your attempt to show that you are reliable; the result will be the opposite. "This individual is not trustworthy; I have to take care". You should never use this technique, other than with the people you know, and you know well. Generally, if you are not a politician seeking to protect your election interest, stay away from this approach, still you can use it through the following strategy:

• **Signing Contracts Strategy.**

Before the customer signs a contract, you can use this method as a message from you to his mind saying: "Dear customer, you have taken the right decision because I and my product are credible". Indeed, he will feel more comfortable after this handshake. You can see a few of the meeting and signing contracts occasions where you discover that they are using this technique of handshaking.

The Dead Fish (Cold and Clammy)

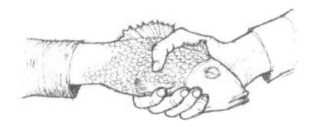

This handshake is special as the hand of the other individual entirely is unwinded, you can imagine if you were holding a dead fish; there is no power in his handshaking, and for that reason, you certainly can control his hand up or down. Your mind will instantly determine that this person is wishy-washy and spineless.

Here, you need to take care of the following:

If you shake hands in this manner, you have to stop because there is no chance for conversation; nobody will appreciate any word you are saying, no one will take your words seriously ever! Some women use this kind of handshake because they are tender, delicate, and fragile, and we need to understand that women can be sensitive and vulnerable. Nobody likes a hard woman or a lady who shakes hands with men intensely. Tenderness does not imply submission, so if you are using this method, you have to raise your handshake strength by one or two levels, but how do you know the degree of the appropriate force? Can the other party take your hand where he wants up or down? If the answer is yes, you need to increase your power over. Practice this at home with a man and a woman. Training with a man is essential since the majority of guys try to loosen their hands when shaking hands with a woman also in order not to be tough on her. Therefore, you should determine handshake strength by feeling if the other party is still able to control your hand with ease.

If the person who shakes hand with you using this method is a client at work, you have to be mindful because any wrong movement by you can put a barrier in front of you from the beginning, so you need to be in full-time concentration throughout the handshake, how? If this client is one of the top classes in the company such as the owner, the General Director of the business, etc. you need to shake hands with him softly and tenderly, do not put pressure on his grasp. Still, your hand needs to be a little tighter and try to have your hand and his in a position of equality, the sides are not upwards (You are controlled) and not downward (you are dominant). In both cases, this makes his mind react instantly, saying to you most of the time 'No', because, as the director of the business, he does not wish to be controlled. If you discover the director shakes hands with this kind of softness and tenderness, then he does not worth to dominate others because he is almost spineless and wishy-washy. So, you are equivalent to him only because he is the director and nothing more. By doing this, he will feel terrific satisfaction from you because you did not encounter location obstacles in front of him as being dominant or controlled. In short, you simply (let it go or leave him alone). You show that you are in control to some extent and, at the same time, make him feel that he is also the dominant! If the client is in a position less than a manager or the authorities, you have to announce immediately to him that you are the source, the greatest, you are Alpha! You are the one that he must rely on and the only option to him. You will make your hand downward and his hand upward; do not pull it, and do not place a significant force in that handshake. Keep it a little bit soft and tender; however you take it to be dominant.

Bone Crushing

This is where you feel a great force on your hand, by the other party as if he is trying to crush your bones. This a trademark of all strong people or those who consider themselves strong.

So, do not use it; never use it with anyone. The strength of your hand ought to be medium and depending upon the situation. Neither keep it extended and unwinded nor tight, remain in the middle always. If you were on the other side, the best way to get rid of the force of the handgrip is that while trying to shake hands with him, get closer to the other party, lowering the distance between you and him, thus decreasing his capability to manage your hand. Doing that, he will not have the ability to increase the force any longer. You have to keep your eyes entirely in his eyes, do not ever blink or look at your hand as he's trying to steal your strength from you, he is checking you, it's a show of power. You will not apply force on his hand, but you will not lose this round with him, so keep your eyes focused on his eyes, continue to smile, a genuine smile indeed. The pain will vanish after a couple of moments, never show that pain to him, and do not look down. Get much closer to him and take a look at him in the face and smile. He will stop. You are at the level with him now, or maybe higher than him, you are the winner in both cases. Don't comment on the strength of his hands, not even by joking, it is over. Carry on with what you are discussing efficiently and quickly.

Hand extended forward

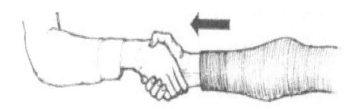

This person says to you, "Please keep away from the personal space!" We'll talk later about the personal space, how to identify it, and how to control it. However he wants you to stay away, and this will be categorised in your mind into two things:

This person is aggressive! Or this individual does not have confidence in himself, and he is more likely to be an Introvert who is afraid of getting near others!

There is something here you and your mind need to see. For people residing in remote villages far from cities, their personal space is higher than the individuals who live in the town because of overcrowding and constant friction in the town, so if we are inhabitants of cities, we get closer to the person we shake hands with.

In contrast, individuals residing in cities do not need to get closer when talking. Therefore, before making conclusions about this person as being an introvert or aggressive, he might becomes from a rural background, nothing more and absolutely nothing less. Surely you should never do it at all circumstances; for you by doing this is forbidden and should not use it to deal with others.

You have your space, and nobody attempts to breach it or break it. So, you are not pressing others far from you, and you will never shake hands with others using this way. If you're the other party, and somebody shakes hands using this method, you'll discover the following:

If the person who is shaking hands with you assumes a higher position in the business as a primary manager or a chairman of the Board of Directors, you will shake him as we have stated previously. You will stay in the space determined by this individual, do not breach, or break his space. He wants you to stay outside it because that would stimulate his mind's rejection guards to be in a standby condition to refuse anything you say or do.

If the individual who is shaking hands with you is a client who remains in a position less than a manager level, you need to know first if you get in his world, would that be better or not for you, but how do you do that? Through the curvature of his body.

If he leans towards you, then he is an individual who appreciates you, but he scared about his personal space, so you need to stay outside it, and at the same time, you need to keep your body in an upright position. Do not lean forward towards him. Considering that your hand is at the top (dominant), you can bend your side a little at the elbow triggering his tight forearm will inevitably flex, making the range between you and him closer. At this moment, you will lean forward towards him and smile. What truly happened is that you are saying to his mind," I'm the dominant! There is no need to fear me, let us get closer to each other, you got to follow my directions, and when we got better, take a look at me I am a safe person."

Here, he will be more relaxed and comfortable because you have proved to him that you are in control; but, you are also reliable and a gentle person.

If his body is leaning away from you, or it is in an upright position, you have to do instead like him; keep your eyes at him, and try to be at the same distance that he is, and do not get closer to him. Keep your body directly and your hand tight, smile! Do not do something else, but to state that you are more powerful. You have to end the handshake, but not him. You can do so by starting to discuss something else and loosen your hand, but beware not to remove your hand, keep it there but open your fingers and relax it silently. We ultimately need to practice to do so efficiently. We need to practice numerous times, and you will master it smoothly, and you will be surprised at its efficiency!

As a woman, for example, if the other person is of the opposite sex! You need to carry out the latter approach, do not enter her space and beware; stay away, but you need to shake hands as the dominant; yes, she wishes to keep you away. However, you do not approach her space because she does not require you to get closer to her world. In this case, her mind will consider you to be polite and trustworthy.

If the other party is a guy: You should also beware of getting closer to him. The majority of men would consider this as a sexual move and will equate this as you like or appreciate him. If you want him, this is good, but if this person is a customer or a client, you have to be careful of using this method because you are not offering yourself here; remember, you are in control.

Getting Fingers

The fingertip grab

Throughout a handshake in many cases, it happens that when people extend their fingers for a handshake, they just do it by mistake in timing. In reality, this does not suggest much. I sometimes try to shake hands with some people, especially some females; they do not extend their full hands on the spot, but merely the fingers. So I have to get her fingers and shake them only and let go instantly. This is because of her internal need to keep herself in the distance comfortable for her. Also, it is due to the different custom and traditions.

A lot of ladies in the world do not usually shake hands with men as they find it awkward to them. Therefore, we have to beware in this regard. If she does not want to shake hands, you need to respect her desire completely.

Understand that a lot of women in our time find it humiliating not to shake hands if a man extends his hand for handshaking.

So she finds herself offering just her fingers due to the social shyness to prevent a guy from feeling ashamed when extending his hand to shake, and the other party does not reciprocate.

Every woman who thinks that she does not need to shake hands with a man; if this is what you believe in, simply refrain from doing it! You are an Alpha person, and the society needs to understand that your values and ideas have to be accepted! If all people around you shake hands, you are ALPHA; what you believe in, you will do, and everyone will appreciate that.

Considering that we are ALPHA, we are not carried away with the mainstream or the existing norms because we are the mainstream, we are the ones who make the mainstream, and we are the ones who run it.

Since the start of humans, the handshake was only restricted to the same gender. Handshaking between the 2 genders was forbidden, other than the partner, the mother or sister, and so on. In today's world, you are instantly beta when a male extended his hand to shake hands with you, why? Because he knows that you initially ought to not handshake him, but since he is dominant, you are now in his world. You will extend your hand to shake his hand. If you do not shake hands with guys,

guys must not do that; however, you have to do it with full respect. When a male extends his hand to shake hands with you, offer him a smile and location your hand on your chest. It is an indication that everyone comprehends and understands. You will find that the male is going to do the same thing right away and puts his hand to his chest, so you are now dominant. You have dragged whoever, even if the person is the only ALPHA worldwide, the most active figure on earth into your world you respectfully, and this is a benefit.

An Exclusive Strategy for Women Only!

It is a technical method at work; use it always, even if you do not have any objection to shaking hands with males. You can reveal that you are an ALPHA person, and you are in control now. Unfortunately, men can refrain from doing that.

Extending a hand for a short range

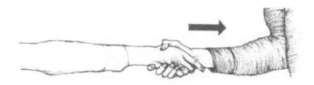

Where a person extends his hand just for a range too short, requiring the other party to extend or bring out his hand to get to shake hands. This is something we all try to do always as much as possible, that is, to reach out a bit where the other party needs to approach you to shake hands with you, therefore entering into your world. You are dominant, for sure.

Use of both hands

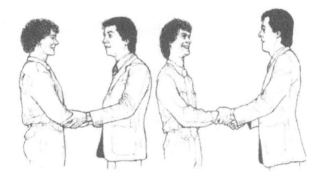

It is done by positioning your left hand either on the wrist, the other party, or on his left lower arm. This will be equated in the mind of who shakes hands in this manner has some new feelings and wishes to make you feel them. Shaking hands with one hand is not sufficient to say what he feels and can not communicate it to the other party by words. You use this way with somebody dear to you too much, or with somebody, you are excited to see him. Try to touch him with as much as you can. Using this with strangers is strictly prohibited!

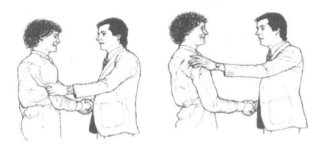

The only case that you can use this method is that if the other party shakes hands with you as a dominant ALPHA individual, and extends his hand to you, you need to go to shake his hand, and you are following his movement. All you need to do is stand beside him or to place your hand on his shoulder or above the elbow. By doing that, you are saying to his mind: "Hello ALPHA, I understand that you are ALPHA, but I'm in charge here." This happens because you positioned your hand on his shoulder, for example, throughout the handshake.

CHAPTER TWO

Manipulation

Brainwashing and hypnosis are the two kinds of manipulation that quickly enters your mind. While these two are essential to comprehending the functioning of manipulation and how it all works, they are not the only options that are offered. Others can be used and are typically more reliable in the brief term than either brainwashing or hypnosis. These specific tactics are ones that can be used in everyday situations, for example, like in typical conversations, an individual may have with others. While it is not likely that a person will be manipulated to change major beliefs through regular discussions, they can be confident to change little things such as being persuaded to purchase cookies from a local girl or to vote a particular way in an election.

The main point to remember about the following three kinds of mind control is that they are most likely to occur in a persons' life with the people that they understand and trust. Indeed, a person is not going to put their subject into seclusion or force them into an altered frame of mind, just like brainwashing. Instead, they will employ various techniques to change the way their subject thinks.

The three kinds of mind control that fit into this category consist of persuasion, manipulation, and deceptiveness.

This chapter is going to go over manipulation and how it can work to change the way "the subject" thinks. While manipulation may not put the individual who is using the method in harms' way, or cause any immediate risk. It can work in a misleading and underhanded way to change the habits, viewpoint, and understanding that the intended subject has in relation to a particular subject or scenario.

What is Manipulation?

The very first question that is asked mostly is, what is manipulation? In this book, we will go over manipulation in terms of mental manipulation, which is a social impact that works to change the behaviors or understanding of others, or the subject, through violent, misleading, or questionable techniques.

The manipulator is going to work to advance their interests, generally at the expense of another, so most of their methods would be seen as deceptive, devious, violent, and exploitative. While mental influence itself is not always negative when an individual or group is being manipulated, it has the possibility of causing them damage.

Mental influence, such as when it comes to a physician working to convince their patients to begin embracing healthy routines, is generally viewed to be something harmless. This is real of any mental influence that is capable of appreciating the right of those allowed to make a choice and is not unduly coercive. On the other hand, if somebody is trying to get their way and is using individuals against their own will, the mental influence can be damaging.

Emotional or mental control is viewed as a kind of persuasion and coercion. Many parts can be added in this form of mind control, such as bullying and brainwashing. For a lot of pieces, individuals will see this as deceptive or abusive.

Those who decide to use manipulation, will do so to control the behavior of those around them. The manipulator will have some objective in mind and will overcome numerous abuse types to coerce those around them into helping the manipulator get to the final goal. Typically emotional blackmail will be included.

Those who practice manipulation will use mind control, brainwashing, or bullying strategies to get others to finish the jobs for them. The subject of the manipulator may not wish to perform the job, but feel that they have no other option due to the blackmail or other method used. Many people who are manipulative lack proper care and sensitivity towards others. So they might not see a problem with their actions.

Other manipulators simply wish to get to their final objective and are not worried about who has been bothered or injured along with the method. Also, because they are scared that others will not accept them, manipulative people are typically scared to get into a healthy relationship. Someone who has a manipulative personality will usually fail to take responsibility for their behaviors, problems, and life. Since they are not able to take responsibility for these concerns, the manipulator will use the methods of manipulation to get someone else to take over the duty.

Manipulators are frequently able to use the same techniques that are found in other types of mind control to get the influence they want over others. One of the most typically used methods is called emotional blackmail. This is where the manipulator will try to influence compassion or regret in the subject they are manipulating. These two emotions are chosen, given that they are considered the two most excellent of all human feelings and are the most likely to spur others into the action that the manipulator wants. The manipulator will then have the ability to take complete advantage of the subject, using the compassion or regret that they have produced to push others into complying or assisting them in reaching their final goal.

Most times, the manipulator will not only be able to develop these emotions, but they also will have the ability to motivate levels of compassion or guilt that are way out of proportion for the circumstance that is going on. This implies that they can take a situation such as missing out on a party appears like the subject is missing out on a funeral service or something significant.

Emotional blackmail is simply among the techniques that are used by manipulators. Among the other strategies that have achieved success for numerous manipulators is to use a type of abuse that is known as mental abuse.

This strategy is usually adopted with the hope of creating insecurity in the subject being controlled; frequently, this insecurity will become so strong that some persons might start to have feelings that they are going nuts. Sometimes, the manipulator will use kinds of passive-aggressive behavior to bring about mental abuse. They may also choose to show support or approval of the subject verbally, but then offer non-verbal hints that reveal different significances. The manipulator will often actively attempt to undermine specific events or habits while showing their support out loud for that same habits. If the manipulator is captured in the act, they will use denial, validation, rationalization, and deception of ill intent to get out of the problem.

Among the most significant issues with mental manipulators is that they are not always able to acknowledge what others around them may need, and they will lose the capability to meet or even consider these needs. This does not excuse the behavior that they are exhibiting. Usually the needs of others are not recognized or are not a top priority to the manipulator, so they can carry out manipulative tasks without feeling guilt or pity. This can make it tough to discuss and stop the behavior in a logical way or why the manipulator needs to stop.

Besides, the manipulator might find that it is tough for them to form significant and long-lasting relationships and because the persons they are with will always feel second hand and will have difficulty in relying on the manipulator. The concern goes both ways in the formation of relationships; the manipulator will not be able to acknowledge the needs of the other individual while the other individual will not be able to form the required emotional connections or trust with the manipulator.

Requirements to Successfully Manipulate

An active manipulator must have tactics at hand that will make them effective at using individuals to get to their last objective. While there are several theories on what makes an active manipulator, we will have a look at the three requirements that have been set out by George K. Simon, a practical psychology author. According to Simon, the manipulator will require:

1. Be able to conceal their aggressive behaviors and intentions from the subject

2. Be prepared to figure out the vulnerabilities of their desired subject or victims to determine which tactics will be the most reliable in reaching their goals.

3. If it comes to that, have some level of ruthlessness easily offered so that they will not require to deal with any doubts that may emerge due to hurting the subjects. This harm can be either physical or psychological.

The very first requirement that the manipulator has to accomplish in order to successfully manipulate their subjects is to conceal their aggressive habits and objectives. No one is going to stick around long enough to be controlled if the manipulator goes around informing everyone their strategies or regularly acts mean to others. Instead, the manipulator needs to have the capability to conceal their thoughts from others and act like everything is normal.

Typically, those who are being controlled will not realize it, at least not in the beginning. The manipulator will be sweet, act as their friends, and perhaps assist them out with one thing or the other. By the time the subject is mindful of the issue, the manipulator has enough details on them to coerce the subject into advancing.

Next, the manipulator will need to have the ability to identify what the vulnerabilities of their intended victim or victims are. This can help them to determine which techniques need to be used to reach the final objective.

Sometimes the manipulator might have the ability to carry out this action through a bit of observation while other times, they are going to need to have some kind of interaction with the subject before creating the full plan.

The third requirement is that the manipulator requires to be callous. It is if the manipulator puts in all their work and then worries about how the subject is going to reasonable in the end, not going to go well. If they did appreciate the issue, it is not most likely that they would be going through with this plan at all. The manipulator is not going to enjoy the subject at all and does not genuinely care if any damage, either physical or psychological, befalls the subject as long as the overall goal is met.

One reason that manipulators are so successful is that the subject typically does not recognize they are being controlled till later at the same time. They might think that whatever is going along only fine; perhaps they feel that they have made a brand-new friend in the manipulator. By the time the subject understands they are being used or no longer desires to be a part of the process, they are stuck. The manipulator will be able to use numerous different methods, consisting of emotional blackmail to get their method completion. How to Control Victims

Among the things that the manipulator requires to be able to achieve to see success is to control their subjects. Several different theories are available to help explain how the manipulator will be able to do this. Two of the techniques that will be discussed in this section include those propounded by Harriet Braiker and Simon.

Harriet Braiker

Harriet Braiker is a clinical psychologist who has written a self-help book. In her writing, she has specified five fundamental ways in which the manipulator can control their subjects. These include:

- **Positive support**
- **Negative support**
- **Intermittent or partial support**

- **Punishment**

- **Traumatic one trial learning**

The very two techniques that are discussed include positive support and negative support. In positive support, the manipulator will use a variety of tactics such as public recognition, facial expressions (like a smile or a forced laugh), attention, presents, approval, money, excessive saying sorry, superficial sympathy which may consist of crocodile tears, superficial charm, and appreciation. The point of using this support is to provide the person with a reason, a wish to be your friend.

They may be more prepared to help you if you give somebody a present or some cash when the time comes out. They will have the required sympathy to be on your side later if you can make the subject feel sorry for you. The other kind of support that can be used is negative support. In this technique, the manipulator will remove the subject from a scenario that is negative as a reward for doing something else. An example of this would be "You won't have to do your homework if you let me to do this to you." Each of these has specific strengths and weaknesses that enable the manipulator to get what they want out of the subject. Often, the manipulator will use a combination of different strategies to get the essential things that they desire.

Intermittent or partial support can also be used by a manipulator. This type of support is used to efficiently create an environment of doubt and fear in the subject. An example of this is available in betting. While the bettor may win sometimes, they are still going to lose some form of money overall, especially if they bet a long time. However, the winning is frequently adequate to keep the subject continuing on the same path, long after they are unable to do so. The manipulator will use this technique to offer support to the subject at sufficient intervals to keep the subject returning.

Punishment is another technique that is used to control the subject of the manipulator. There are a lot of different actions that can fit into this classification. They include playing the subject, weeping, sulking, using the regret trip, emotional blackmail, swearing, risks, and intimidation, using the quiet treatment, shouting, and nagging. The point of using this technique is to make the subject seem like they have done something wrong. The subject will feel bad and wish to make things right, falling right back in with the manipulator.

The last method that Braiker mentions in her work is traumatic one-trial learning. This is where the manipulator will explode for the smallest things in the hopes of conditioning or training the subject into not wanting to oppose, challenge, or upset the manipulator. Some of the tactics that may be used in this method include explosive anger, spoken abuse, and other habits that are frightening and used to establish supremacy and dominance over the subject.

Simon

Simon has also come up with a list of strategies that manipulators should use to manage their victims successfully. A few of these resemble those noted by Braiker but with some more details.

These would include:

Lying: Manipulators are proficient at lying to their subjects. Often, the subjects will discover that it is tough to tell when they are being lied to at the time. When the subject finds out about the evident lie, it usually is too late to do anything about it. The only manner in which the subject can make sure that they are minimizing their chances of being lied to is keeping an eye out for different personality types that are professionals in the art of cheating and lying. The manipulator will lie about anything to get their method, and for the parts, their subjects will not have any idea of going on up until it is far too late to do anything about it.

Omission lying: this one resembles the method listed above with a few small differences omission lying is a bit more subtle because the manipulator will say a little of the truth but will keep certain vital issues that should have been exposed. In many cases, this might be called propaganda. The manipulator may say that they need to borrow some money to go purchase groceries when, in reality, they need the cash to go pick up some drugs or other prohibited items. While they did use the money to purchase groceries as they said, they excluded a vital part. If they understood the end of the story and now they may be caught up in something, the subject probably would not have offered the cash prohibited.

Denial: Manipulators are experts at rejection. None will confess that they have done something wrong, even when all of the proof is pointing towards them. They will always deny everything and often make the subject seem the one at fault.

Justification: This is when the manipulator will make up an excuse that makes them look good. They may say they only did the act because they were trying to help the subject. This tactic is also related to the strategy of spinning.

Reduction: This is a blend of denial and rationalization techniques. The manipulator will tell everybody that their habits are not as hazardous or reckless as the subject thinks when the manipulator states that an insult or tease they carried out was simply a joke and that the subject needs not to take it so seriously.

Selective attention or inattention: During this strategy, the manipulator works to prevent giving care to anything that will distract them from their last goal. They will trivialize it and make it appear not that important to them, which it truly isn't. An example of this would be when the manipulator says, "I do not wish to hear it."

Diversion: manipulators are not only good at lying to their subjects; they are also professionals at avoiding offering straight responses to questions that are provided to them. If somebody asks them a question that they do not like or would like to know outright if they are lying to them, the manipulator will try to press the conversation in another direction. Frequently the manipulator will quickly provide an unclear answer to the question before moving the discussion to another subject.

Evasion: This technique is very similar to diversion with a few distinctions. In this tactic, the manipulator will address the questions that are given to them, but they will use weird words, unclear actions, rattle on and provide inappropriate responses to the question. They will leave the subject with more questions than answers when they are done.

Intimidation: The manipulator will always attempt to keep the victim on the defensive to make sure that they remain on the same team throughout the procedure. Frequently this is done by using veiled, implied, indirect, or subtle threats to the subject.

Regret Trip: manipulators like to use the guilt journey as a form of intimidation to get them based on doing what they desire. The manipulator will try to make the subject feel guilty in some method, such as by stating that the subject has it too simple, is too self-centered, or simply does not care about the manipulator enough. This will lead to the victim starting to feel bad for the manipulator. The subject will then be kept in a submissive, nervous, or self-doubting position, making it much easier for the manipulator to use them still.

Shaming: The entire goal of the manipulator is to make the subject feel bad or have sympathy for them so that the subject keeps supporting the plan. A manner in which the manipulator does this is using sarcasm to pity the subject. This method will make the subject feel not worthy. Many of the shaming strategies used will be subtle and would consist of things such as subtle sarcasm, rhetorical remarks, undesirable tone of voice, or an intense look.

Playing as a victim: No matter what, the manipulator wants to look like he is the victim, even though he's the one in control. When the manipulator imitates, they are the victim of their scenarios or the behavior of another person; they will be able to stimulate pity, sympathy, and empathy. The majority of people will not be able to stand by and watch as somebody suffers, and the manipulator will find that it is simple to get these same people to comply with them.

Damning the subject: This is one of the most effective strategies that can be used because it will immediately put the subject on the function of defence while at the same time it hides the manipulator's aggressive intents. The manipulator will try to turn the situations around, so that the subject may appear as the villain. The subject will then wish to find ways to change this outlook and get on the side of the manipulator once again, making it simple to be used.

Servant role: Manipulators will frequently hide their programs by making it look like the work they are doing is for some worthy cause. They just stated the mean aspect of your attire because the primary wishes to start sprucing up the look of the school, and they wanted to assist. The term "just doing my job," would likewise fit under this classification.

Seduction: Manipulators can use seduction to get the things that they desire. Some tools that fit into this classification would include strong support, appreciation, beauty, and flattery. This is carried out to get the subject to reduce their defences. After a time, the subject will begin to give their commitment and trust to the manipulator who will use it as they please.

Projecting the blame: The manipulator will spend a lot of time blaming others for the issues they have. Typically it is challenging to identify when this is going on, so no one can call them out on it.

Feigning innocence: If the manipulator is caught in the act of reaching their plan, they will attempt to suggest that if the damage was done, it was unintended. They might even totally deny that they did anything in the very first place. When caught, the manipulator will place a look of anger or surprise on their faces. The point of this tool is to make the victim question their peace of mind and judgment because it looks like they were wrong.

Feigning confusion: Another thing that may take place if the manipulator is captured is that they may play dumb. This will take place if the manipulator attempts to pretend that they do not have any idea what the subject is saying. When a vital concern is brought up to them, they may likewise act like they are puzzled.

Brandishing anger: when the manipulator uses violence, it is to get the subject to regret or compassion for them. If carried out in the right method, the manipulator will have the ability to shock their subject back into submission. Frequently, the manipulator is not truly mad; they are merely placing on an act to get what they desire.

As can be seen, there is a lot of tools that the manipulator can use to get to their final objectives. Typically, these methods will be used in such a way that the subject will not understand what is going on at the start, and it will take a while for them to catch on. Once they do, the manipulator will be able to use some of the strategies that will be gone over in the next area to keep the subject going in the ideal direction. The manipulator is competent at using a combination of these skills to get the things that they desire, and it does not matter to them how much they hurt the other person while doing so.

Strategies of Manipulation

As discussed before, a manipulator is going to operate to reach their last objective. To achieve this final goal, the manipulator will use any method that they can to get people to do what they desire. The five most common ways that will be used by a manipulator to reach their final goals consist of blackmail, emotional blackmail, putting down the other person, lying, and producing an illusion. These will each be gone over in the preceding sections.

Blackmail

Blackmail is the first strategy that would be used by a manipulator. Blackmail is considered an act that includes dangers that are unjustified to make a specific gain or cause a loss to the subject unless the manipulator's demand is met. It can also be defined as the act of coercion that involves threats of prosecution as a criminal, hazards of taking the subject's home or cash, or risks of triggering physical harm to the subject.

For this blackmail is more of a hazard, either physical or emotional to the subject to coerce them into doing what the manipulator wants.

Blackmail is also considered extortion in some cases. There are times when the two are considered related; there are some differences. Extortion is when someone takes the individual property of another by threatening to do future harm if the property is not given.

On the other hand, blackmail is when threats are used to avoid the subject from participating in legal activities. At times, these two occasions are going to work together. The individual may threaten someone and need money to be kept at bay and not trigger the subject damage.

The manipulator is going to have the ability to use this strategy to get what they desire. They are going to take the time to find out things of personal nature about their subject, and then they can use that as a type of blackmail against them. They may blackmail their subject by threatening to spill an embarrassing secret or by ruining their chances of getting a new job or promotion. Or the manipulator may work enormously by threatening to physically damage their subject or the subject's household if they do not consent to accompany the manipulator. Whatever the blackmail may be, it is used to help the manipulator to get to their final goal with the support of the subject.

Emotional Blackmail

Another similar technique that may be used by the manipulator is known as emotional blackmail. Throughout this strategy, the manipulator will find ways to influence sympathy or guilt in their subject. These two emotions are the strongest ones for human beings to feel, and they will typically suffice to stimulate the subject into the action that the manipulator wants. The manipulator is going to take benefit of this fact to get the thing that they desire; they will use the compassion or the regret that they influence to push the subject in to cooperating or assisting them. The degree of empathy or regret will frequently be exaggerated, making the subject a lot likely to help out in the scenario.

The point of using this kind of blackmail is to play more on the feelings of the subject. In regular blackmail, the subject has a risk to deal with, mainly in terms of physical harm to themselves or someone they enjoy. With psychological blackmail, the manipulator will work to motivate feelings that are strong enough to prompt the based on action. While the subject may think that they are helping in their own free will, the manipulator has worked to guarantee that the subject is helping and will highlight the emotions again whenever it is required.

Putting Down The Other Person

There are other options readily available to the manipulator if they would like to get their subject to help in reaching the final objective. One method that has a bit of success instead is when the manipulator can put down their subject.

In most cases, if the manipulator uses verbal abilities to put their subject down, they will run a high risk of making the subject feel as if a personal attack has been placed on them. When the subject feels like they are assaulted, they will bristle and not be ready to the manipulator in the manner in which they want. Instead, the subject will not like the manipulator and will remain as far away from them as possible, making it extremely tough for the manipulator to reach their final objective.

This is why the manipulator is not going to walk around and put down their subject simply. They have to be more discreet about the process and find a way to do it without raising warnings or making the subject feel like they are being assaulted. One manner in which this can be done is through humour. Humour can lower barriers that might otherwise appear because humour is funny and makes people feel good. The manipulator can turn their insult into a joke. Even though the insult has become a joke, it will work only as if the trick were not present without leaving the visible scars on the subject.

Often, the manipulator will direct their insult to a third person if it comes back to haunt them later on. This helps them to mask what they are saying more quickly along with providing an easy way to deny causing damage. They may start their insult with "Other people think ..." If the subject is still able to think that the comments were made at them, then the manipulator would end it with a throwaway line that may consist of something like "present company excepted, of course."

The idea of the insult is to make the subject feel like they are in some way less than the manipulator. It raises the manipulator as much as a new level and leaves the subject feeling like something is missing. The subject is more likely to wish to make things much better and to fix any wrong that they have done.

Lying

No matter what the final objective of the manipulator is, lying is something that they are an expert in and which they will do all of the time to get what they want. Several kinds of lies can be used by the manipulator that will help them to reach their goals. One is that they tell mostly lies, and others consist of leaving out parts of the truth from their subjects.

When the manipulator lies, it is because they know that the lie is going to enhance their plan much more successfully than the truth would. Telling somebody the reality may make them not desire to help the manipulator out which would go entirely against their strategies. Instead, the manipulator will tell lies to get the subject convinced to do something for them, and by the time the subject discovers the deception, it will be too late to fix the issue.

The manipulator may also decide to leave out part of the truth in the stories that they are telling. With this method, they are going to say parts of the fact but will keep specific things out, which may prevent the progress that is being made. These kinds of lies can be just as hazardous because it will become increasingly challenging to say what the reality of the story is and what the lie is.

It is essential to understand that when you are handling the manipulator, anything that they inform you might be a lie. It is not a great concept to trust anything that the manipulator is saying since they are merely trying to abuse and use their subjects to reach that last goal. The manipulator is going to do and say anything possible, even lying, to get what they want, and they are not going to regret it. As long as they get what they desire, they are not too concerned about how it is impacting the subject or others around them. Thereby creating an illusion

In addition to lying, the manipulator is going to be an expert at creating impressions that are capable of bringing about their final goal better. They will work to develop an image that they desire and then convince the subject that this impression is real, whether it does not matter to the manipulator. The manipulator will create the proof that is needed to achieve this. The manipulator will plant the idea and the evidence into the minds of the subject.

As soon as these ideas are in place, the manipulator will have the ability to step back for a couple of days and let the manipulation occur in the mind of the subject overtime. After that time, the manipulator will have more chance of getting the subject to go with the plan.

Manipulation is a type of mind control that is challenging for the subject to prevent. Unlike brainwashing and hypnosis that was described in the previous chapters, manipulation can take place in everyday life. In some instances, it can occur without the subject having much understanding or control of it.

The manipulator is going to work discretely to reach their final objective without getting the subject suspicious and thwart the procedure. The manipulator will not worry about who they are injuring or how others might feel, and most of them are not capable of comprehending the needs of their subjects. They feel in one's bones that they desire something and that the subject they have picked is going to assist them in getting to their goal.

The techniques discussed in this chapter are to help describe what goes on during the process of manipulation. It is usually best to try to stay away from anyone who may be a manipulator so that you can avoid this type of mind control.

Ins and out of manipulation psychology

Manipulative psychology gets a lousy press right from the start. After all, the very words used to explain it suggest that you'll be manipulating someone or something, and that's rarely a popular choice with other individuals. So, there are numerous questions to be addressed. The primary ones are "what the heck is manipulative psychology?" and "should I use it?".

In a nutshell, manipulative psychology is the art of getting your way. Kids are good at this, but we lose the ability to get our way as we age - and as other individuals get better to what we're doing.

So manipulative psychology puts a kind of skin around the essential things we do to increase the effectiveness and also minimize the detection rate. And, when you think about it, those two work together. If people do not understand that you're swaying their deeds and ideas, then you're more likely to get the preferred outcome from them.

One way that we get manipulated all the time is with the "knowledge of the crowds" It's a bit like asking the audience on the quiz program Who Wants To Be A Millionaire? The hope is that, on balance, the joint decision is the best one.

Websites like Amazon use this to manipulate us all the time. The results they reveal are often in the order of popularity and regularly have the most evaluations. Many of those reviews will be from genuine individuals like you and me. But a few of them might be sneakier efforts to get you to buy a product - it's not unheard of for a few of the reviews to be paid for. There have likewise been cases of individuals trying to press down a rival's product by leaving negative reviews. That's one genuine world case where manipulative psychology is used regularly, even though it's not a situation that's generally quoted.

Another common usage of manipulative psychology is to turn it into reverse psychology. We use this on our kids a lot. For instance, when we tell them to eat their vegetables, otherwise they won't grow up to be big and robust. Or - even sneakier - when we state that they don't have to do something in the complete knowledge that they will rebel against the declaration and do whatever it was that we wanted them to do in the very first place.

That trick works with older people too, not just children. It is excellent in an argument as you can huff and puff and say things that force the other individual to take your views, even though they would just do that in the heat of the moment.

Perhaps a preferred way of using this sort of manipulative psychology is by planting the seed of an idea in somebody else's mind. This requires a bit of planning but works well. You say something in passing in such a manner in which the other individual's brain will just grab onto it and keep it away.

Over the next few days or weeks, their mind will play with the idea, and then unexpectedly, out of the blue, they'll develop the idea you first considered - except that they'll declare it as their own.

CHAPTER THREE

Mind Control

Mind control is a concept that has captivated individuals for many years. Stories have been told by the media and in films about groups of people who have been brainwashed or hypnotized into doing things they would never do otherwise. There are individuals on both sides of the issue; some believe that there is no such thing as mind control, that it is all just imagined while others believe that they could be manipulated by mind control anytime.

This chapter will discuss a few of the different types of mind control, how they work, and whether they can have an everyday life application.

Kinds of Mind Control

The idea of mind control has been around for several years now. If someone were able to control their minds and make them do things against their will, people have had both fascinations and worry about what would take place.

Conspiracy theories run plentiful about government authorities and other individuals of power using their skills to control what little groups of individuals are doing. Even in some lawsuits, some defendants have raised it as the reason why they committed criminal acts. Despite the drama of mind control that has been portrayed in the media, there is little understanding of the kinds of mind control and how each of them works. This chapter will check out a bit about the most common types of mind control as a way of explaining more about this exciting subject.

While various types of mind control can be used to control the intended victim, there are five that are most frequently considered. These consist of brainwashing, hypnosis, deceptiveness, manipulation, and persuasion. These will all be discussed below:

Brainwashing

Brainwashing is the very first type of mind control to talk about. It is generally the process where somebody will be convinced to abandon beliefs that they had in the past to take new values and standards. There are a lot of ways that this can be done, although not all of them will be thought about bad. If you are from an African country and then move to America, you will typically be required to change your values and ideals to fit in with the new culture and environments that you find yourself. On the other hand, for those in concentration camps, when a new dictator government is taking over, they will often go through the process of brainwashing to convince residents to follow along quietly.

Many individuals have misunderstandings of what brainwashing is. Some people have more paranoid ideas about the practice, including mind control devices that are sponsored by the federal government, which are thought to be easily used just like a remote control. On the other side of things, some skeptics do not believe that brainwashing is possible at all and that anyone who claims it has happened is lying. For the many parts, the practice of brainwashing will land someplace in the middle of these two ideas.

During the practice of brainwashing, the subject will be persuaded to alter their beliefs about something through a combination of different techniques. There is not just one technique that can be used throughout this procedure, so it can be tough to put the practice into a neat little box. For a lot of parts, the subject will be separated from all of the essential things that they know. From there, they will be broken down into an emotion that makes them susceptible before the new concepts are introduced. As the subject absorbs this new details, they will be rewarded for expressing ideas and thoughts which support these originalities. The reward is what will be used to enhance the brainwashing that is taking place.

Brainwashing is not new to the society. Individuals have been using these methods for a very long time. In a historical context, those who were prisoners of war were often brainwashed before being convinced to change sides. Some of the most compelling cases of these would lead to the prisoner becoming an extremely fervent convert to the new position. These practices were unique in the beginning and would usually be imposed depending upon who supervised. In time, the term of brainwashing was established, and some more strategies were presented to make the practice more universal.

The more modern methods would depend on the field of psychology, given that a lot of those concepts were used to demonstrate how people might change their minds through persuasion.

A lot of actions go along with the brainwashing process. It is not something that is going to just happen to you when you walk down the street and speak to someone that you have only met. One of the primary requirements that come with brainwashing being active is that the subject must be kept in seclusion. If the subject can be around other people, they will learn how to think as usual and the brainwashing will not be reliable at all.

When the subject is in isolation, they will go through a process that is adopted to break down their self-esteem. They are told that all the things they know are incorrect and are made to feel like whatever they do is wrong. After months of going through all of this, the subject will seem like they are wrong, and the regret is going to overwhelm them. Once they have reached this point, the agent will begin to lead them towards the new belief system and identity that is desired. The subject will be directed to think that the new options are all their own and so it is more likely to stick.

The whole process of brainwashing can take many months to even years. It is not something that is going to happen in just a discussion, and for the most part, it will not be able to occur beyond prison camps and a few isolated cases.

Mostly, those who go through brainwashing have done so when someone is trying to persuade them of a new perspective. For example, if you remain in an argument with a friend and they encourage you that their ideas make good sense, you have technically gone through brainwashing. Sure, it may not be evil, and you were able to consider all of it logically, but you were still encouraged to change the beliefs that you held previously. It is sporadic that someone undergoes real brainwashing, where they will have their entire value system replaced. It will typically happen throughout the process of occurring to a new point of view, despite whether the strategies used were persuasive or not.

CHAPTER FOUR

Hypnosis

While brainwashing is a widely known form of mind control and manipulation that lots of people have heard of, hypnosis is also an essential type that needs to be considered. For a lot of parts, those who are familiar with hypnosis know about it from seeing phase programs of participants doing senseless acts. While this is a kind of hypnosis, there is a lot more to it. This chapter is going to concentrate more on hypnosis as a type of mind control and manipulation.

What is Hypnosis?

To start with is the definition of hypnosis. According to experts, hypnosis is considered a state of consciousness that involves the concentrated attention in addition to the minimized peripheral awareness that is identified by the participant's increased capacity to respond to suggestions that are provided. This means that the individual is going to get in a different state of mind, and will be more prone to following the ideas that are offered by the hypnotherapist.

It is commonly known that two theory groups help to explain what is taking place throughout the hypnosis period. The first one is referred to as the modified state theory. Those who follow this theory see that hypnosis resembles a trance or a mindset that is changed where the participant will see that their awareness is somewhat different from what they would see in their normal conscious state. The other theory is the non-state theories. The followers of this theory do not believe that those who go through hypnosis are getting into a different state of consciousness. Instead, the person is dealing with the hypnotist to go into a kind of imaginative role enactment.

While in hypnosis, the participant is believed to have more concentration and focus that couples together with a new ability to focus extremely on a particular memory or thought. During this process, the individual is also able to shut out other sources that might be distracting to them. The hypnotized subjects are believed to show a heightened ability to react to suggestions that are offered to them, mainly when these ideas originate from the hypnotherapist. The process that is used to position an individual into hypnosis is referred to as hypnotic induction and will involve a series of recommendations and guidelines that are used as a kind of heat up.

Various ideas are brought up by the professionals as to what the meaning of hypnosis is. The broad range of these meanings originates from the fact that there are so many scenarios that involve hypnosis, and nobody has the same experience when they are going through it. Some of the different definitions of hypnosis by specialists consist of the following:

1. "A unique case of psychological regression," *Michael Nash*.

2. Ernest Hilgard and Janet Hilgard have written in great depth about hypnosis and explain it has a method for the body to dissociate from itself in another level of awareness.

3. Sarbin and Coe, two well-known social psychologists, have to use the term of role theory to explain hypnosis. Under this definition, the participant is playing the function of being hypnotized. They act like they are hypnotized instead of being in that state.

4. According to T.X. Barber, hypnosis is defined based on the different no hypnotic behavioural criteria. Under this definition, the individual will specify the work motivation and label the

circumstance that they are in as hypnosis, given that they have no other thing to call it.

5. Weitzenhoffer wrote in a few of his earlier works about hypnosis. He conceived that hypnosis is a state of enhanced suggestibility. In more current engagement, he went on to specify the act of hypnosis as "a form of impact by a single person applied to another through the medium or firm of suggestion.

6. Brenman and Gill used the psychoanalytic principle of "regression in the service of the ego" to help describe what hypnosis was all about. Under this meaning, the participant wants to go under hypnosis and into the modified state because it helps out their ego and makes them feel better.

7. According to Edmonston, an individual who has gone through hypnosis is merely in a deep state of relaxation.

8. Spiegel and Spiegel have stated that hypnosis is hardly something that takes place because of the biological capability of the participant.

9. Erickson mentions that hypnosis is a transformed, inner-directed, and unique state of operating. The individual is still

able to work and is conscious of things around them; however, they are in an altered state compared to their normal state.

Some various views and declarations have been made about hypnosis. Some people believe that hypnosis is genuine and are paranoid that the federal government and others around them will try to control their minds. Others do not believe in hypnosis at all and think that it is merely a deception. The idea of hypnosis as mind control falls somewhere in the middle.

There are three stages of hypnosis that are acknowledged by the psychological community. These three stages include induction, idea, and vulnerability. Each of them is very important to the hypnosis process and will be discussed below.

Induction

The very first phase of hypnosis is induction. Before the individual goes through the full hypnosis, they will be presented to the hypnotic induction strategy. For many years, this was believed to be the approach used to put the subject into their hypnotic trance. But that definition has changed in modern times. A few of the non-state theorists have seen this phase slightly in a different way. Instead, they see this phase as the approach to increase the participants' expectations of what is going to happen, defining the function that they will play, getting their attention to focus in the best direction and any of the other actions that are needed to lead the individual into the ideal instructions for hypnosis.

Several induction methods can be used throughout hypnosis. The most famous and popular methods are Braid's "eye-fixation" strategy or "Braidism." There are instead a few variations of this approach, including the Stanford Hypnotic Susceptibility Scale (SHSS). This scale is the most used tool for research in the field of hypnosis.

To use the Braid induction techniques, you will need to follow a couple of steps. The first one is to take any object that you can find that is intense, such as a watch case, and hold it in between the fore thumb and middle fingers on the left hand. You will wish to hold this item about 8 - 15 inches from the eyes of the individual. Hold the thing somewhere above the forehead to produce a lot of strain on the eyelids, and eyes throughout the process so that the participant can keep a fixed stare on the item at all times.

The hypnotist should then describe to the person that they should keep their eyes fixed continuously on to the object. The patient will also need to focus their mind entirely on the idea of that specific item. They need not be allowed to think of other things or let their brains and eyes roam; else, the process will not succeed.

After a brief time, the individual's eyes will begin to dilate. With a bit more time, the participant will start to presume an undulating movement. They are in the trance if the participant involuntarily closes their eyelids when the middle. And forefingers of the ideal hand are brought from the eyes to the things. If not, then the individual will require to start once again.

Ensure to let the individual know that they are to allow their eyes to close, and then the fingers are brought in a comparable movement back towards the eyes again. This will get the patient to go into the changed mindset, which is called hypnosis.

While Braid waited for his method, he did acknowledge that using the induction method of hypnosis is not needed continuously for every case. Scientists in contemporary times have usually found that the induction method is not as crucial to the impacts of a hypnotic idea as formerly believed. With time, other alternatives and variations of the original hypnotic induction method have been developed, although the Braid approach is still seen as the best.

Suggestion

The next stage of hypnosis is known as the suggestion phase. When hypnosis was very first described by James Braid, the term of guidance was not used. Instead, Braid referred to this stage as the act of having the mind of the individual focus on one central and dominant idea. How Braid did it was to stimulate or minimize the physiological functioning of the areas on the participant's body. Later on, Braid started to position more and more focus on making use of various non-verbal and spoken forms of an idea to get the individual into the hypnotic mindset. These would consist of using "waking ideas" in addition to self-hypnosis. Another widely known hypnotist, Hippolyte Bernheim, continued to shift the emphasis of the physical state of the process of hypnosis over to the mental process, which contained verbal tips.

According to Bernheim, hypnotherapy is the induction of a psychical condition that is strange, which will increase the vulnerability of the suggestion to the individual. Typically, he stated, the hypnotic state that is induced will help with the idea, even though this might not be required to start the vulnerability in the first place.

Modern hypnotherapy uses a lot of different suggestion forms to achieve success, such as metaphors, insinuations, non-verbal or indirect tips, direct verbal ideas, and other figures of speech and thoughts that are non-verbal. A few of the non-verbal suggestions that may be used throughout the suggestion stage would consist of physical manipulation, voice tonality, and mental imagery.

Among distinctions made in the types of suggestions that can be provided to the participant includes those suggestions that are provided with consent and those that are more authoritarian.

Things to be thought about, in regards to hypnosis, is the distinction between the unconscious and the conscious mind. Numerous therapists see the phase of suggestion as a method of communicating, directed for the many parts to the conscious mind of the subject. Others in the field will see it in the different instructions; they see the interaction happening between the agent and the unconscious mind.

Advocates of the first class of thought included Bernheim, Braid, and other leaders of the Victorian age. They thought the suggestions were being resolved straight to the mindful part of the subject's mind, instead of to the unconscious part. Braid goes even more and in fact, specifies the act of hypnotherapy as the concentrated attention upon the suggestion or the dominant concept. The fear of the people that therapists can enter into their unconscious and make them believe things beyond their control is severe, according to those who follow this train of idea.

The nature of the mind has also been the determinant of the various conceptions about the recommendation. Those who thought that the actions provided are through the unconscious mind, such as in the case of Milton Erickson, bring up examples of using indirect tips. Numerous of these indirect ideas, such as metaphors or stories, will hide their desired significance to disguise it from the conscious mind of the subject.

A subliminal tip is a form of hypnosis that relies entirely on the theory of the unconscious mind; if the unconscious mind were not being used in hypnosis, this sort of suggestion would not be possible. The differences between the two groups are fairly simple to recognize; those who believe that the tips will go primarily to the conscious mind will use direct spoken guidelines and ideas. Those who think the ideas will go mostly to the unconscious mind will use stories and metaphors with covert meanings.

In either of these theories of ideas, the individual will need to be able to focus on one object or an idea. This enables them to be led in the direction that is required to enter into the hypnotic state. Once the suggestion stage has been finished, the participant can move into the third phase, vulnerability.

Vulnerability

Over time, it has been observed that people will react in a different way to hypnosis. Some individuals discover that they can fall into a hypnotic trance relatively quickly and do not need to put much effort into the process at all. Others may find that they can enter into the hypnotic trance, but just after a prolonged period and with some effort. Still, others will find that they are unable to enter into the hypnotic trance, and even after continued efforts will not reach their goals. One thing that researchers have discovered intriguing about the vulnerability of different participants is that this aspect remains consistent. If you could quickly get into a hypnotic frame of mind, you are most likely to be the same method for the rest of your life. On the other hand, if you have consistently had trouble in reaching the hypnotic state and have never been hypnotized, then it is likely that you never will.

There have been several different designs developed gradually to attempt and determine the susceptibility of participants to hypnosis. Some of the older depth scales worked to presume which level of hypnotic trance the participant was in through the observable indications that were available. These would include things such as spontaneous amnesia. Some of the more modern-day scales work to measure the degree of self-evaluated or observed responsiveness to the particular recommendation tests that are offered, such as the direct suggestions of arm rigidness.

According to the research that has been done by Deirdre Barrett, there are two types of subjects considered susceptible to the results of hypnotherapy. These two groups include dissociates and fantasizers.

The fantasizers will score high on the absorption scales, can quickly shut out the stimuli of the real world without using hypnosis, spend a lot of their time daydreaming, had fictional friends when they were a child. Also, they grew up in an environment where imaginary play was motivated.

On the other side of things are dissociates. This group will often come from a background of trauma or youth abuse, found methods to forget the unpleasant events that remain in their past, and can escape into a tingling, if a person in this group does daydream, it is more in regards to going blank instead of developing fantasies. Both of these groups scored high on the tests of hypnotic susceptibility. The two groups that have the greatest rates of hypnotisability include those experiencing posttraumatic stress disorder and dissociative identity condition.

Forms

Hypnosis, as a field and as an idea, has been around for a very long time. Due to this, various forms have started to emerge that help in putting the process of hypnosis to good usage. The different forms of using hypnosis cross many fields such as home entertainment, self-improvement, military usages and medical uses. Other locations that have just recently started to use hypnotism include rehabilitation, physical therapy, education, sports, and forensics. Even artists have begun to use hypnotism to reach specific creative purposes. This is revealed the most by Andre Breton, a surrealist artist who has used hypnosis amongst other strategies for his artistic goals. Among the growing uses of hypnosis remains in the field of self-improvement; lots of people have picked to do self-hypnosis to help them slim down, lower tension, and quit smoking.

The following areas will go over some different fields where hypnosis is growing with how the procedure of hypnosis is working in those fields. Hypnotherapy.

Hypnotherapy is making use of hypnosis as a type of psychotherapy. It is used as an approach to assist the client or subject through unpleasant problems that are afflicting them, especially when other methods of self-discipline are not efficient. Certified psychologists and physicians may carry out a type of hypnotherapy on prepared clients to assist them in treating posttraumatic tension, compulsive gaming, sleep conditions, eating conditions, stress and anxiety, and anxiety.

It is also possible to approve a certified hypnotherapist to help you in dealing with problems such as weight management and the cessation of cigarette smoking. If you go to a licensed hypnotherapist, it is essential to bear in mind that they are not psychologists or physicians, so they will just have the ability to assist you with reaching the hypnotic state and not with treating your more significant conditions. You should ensure whoever you are dealing with has been certified to supply you with these services, whether you select a hypnotherapist or a physician.

The procedure of hypnotherapy has been seen in various forms in modern-day history. All of them have had differing degrees of success, depending on the issue dealt with and the individuals.

A few of the kinds that have been used include:

Cognitive-behavioral hypnotherapy: this is a mix of scientific hypnosis along with various aspects of the Cognitive-Behavioral Therapy.

Hypnoanalysis: this is also referred to as age regression hypnotherapy:

- hypnosis to help with handling worries and fears

- Ericksonian hypnotherapy

Hypnotherapy:

 - to assist with addictions

- to assist with habit control

- to assist with pain management in those who experience persistent pain

- to help in the mental therapy the client is currently dealing with

- to assist with relaxation

- to help with skin diseases

- to assist with calming clients who are nervous about going through surgical treatment.

- to help with the efficiency of athletes before competitors

- to assist with weight loss

Military Applications

In addition to helping people who deal with various health concerns and dependency, individuals have long wondered if governmental and military officials have used hypnosis to change the method residents consider things. Far, there has been little proof that the American military is capable or has used hypnosis to reach their goals. A declassified file that was obtained out of flexibility of the Information Act archive recently shows that the procedure of hypnosis has been investigated for the use in military applications. Despite the research done, the study concluded that there indeed wasn't any evidence that the process of hypnosis would be beneficial in a military application. Also, there was no evidence that clearly showed that hypnosis exists in relation to an actual phenomenon outside of subject span, great inspiration, and reasonable suggestion.

The file further goes on to describe how it would be almost impossible for hypnosis to be used in a military application. It states: "The use of hypnosis in intelligence would present particular technical problems not encountered in the center or lab to acquire compliance from a resistant source. For instance, it would be required to hypnotize the source under basically hostile situations. There is no competent evidence, speculative or scientific, that this can be done." The document explains that it has been hard to study the impacts, and application of hypnosis to be used in the military. Because no one can say with certainty whether hypnosis is a unique state with some conditioned reactions or just a type of idea that has been caused as a result of the favorable relationship between the subject and the hypnotherapist. Self-hypnosis.

There are some instances, such as when a qualified hypnotherapist or other professional is not available, when you may decide to use the process of self-hypnosis. This procedure happens when an individual can hypnotize themselves, frequently using the strategy of autosuggestion. The primary use for this technique is for self-improvement, and lots of individuals will perform it to lower their stress levels, quit smoking cigarettes, or getting the inspiration they need to go on a diet.

While some individuals may have the ability to self-hypnotize themselves, numerous discover that they need some sort of assistance in reaching the transformed state. This might include hypnotic recordings or even mind device gadgets to help them achieve that state. Other areas that you could use self-hypnosis for include your overall physical well-being, to relax, and to overcome phase fright.

Stage Hypnosis

When many people think about hypnosis, they think about stage hypnosis. This is a kind of entertainment that occurs in a theatre or a club in front of an audience. The hypnotist is often shown as an excellent showman, and this helps in encouraging the idea that hypnosis is totally about mind control. At the beginning of the act, the therapist will attempt to put the entire audience under the altered state before selecting certain people who satisfy the requirements to come upon the phase and go through different awkward acts. At the same time, the remainder of the group watches.

It is unknown why phase hypnosis is so reliable, although it is often believed to be a combination of trickery, stagecraft, physical control, suggestibility, participant choice, and mental aspects. For many parts, experts believe the participant is playing along with the hypnotist and providing an excellent show. These people may want to do this because they want to be in the middle of all the attention, the pressure to please others and the excuse to go against their suppressors of fear make it simple to get the participants to carry out. Some of the books that have been composed by former stage therapists reinforce the concept of hoax and deceptiveness, and some are entirely composed of fake hypnosis where private whispers were used the entire time.

Kinds of Hypnosis

There are many types of hypnosis that the subject will be able to undergo. Each of them will operate in slightly various ways, and a few of them work to assist with different problems. Some might be more fit to helping the subject to relax while others can assist more with weight loss or pain management. This section will talk in more information about the various types of hypnosis that are readily available.

Conventional Hypnosis

The most common kind of hypnosis used is referred to as conventional hypnosis. During this procedure, the agent merely is making suggestions straight to the subject's unconscious mind. This kind of hypnosis will work the best on a subject which is understood for accepting the things that they are informed, and they do not ask a lot of concerns. You will be going through the process of conventional hypnosis if you go and visit a certified hypnotist or acquire a tape to do the process of self-hypnosis because it does not take that much experience or training to find out how to do. This is the reason that this type of hypnosis is so popular. The hypnotherapist is just going to have to write a basic script and tell the subject what to do. While this strategy will work exceptionally well on those who accept what is going on around them. It is inefficient for those who believe critically and analytically.

Ericksonian Hypnosis

The next kind of hypnosis to be discussed is Ericksonian Hypnosis. This one is a bit more in-depth because it is going to require making use of metaphors and little stories. These are used to provide the concepts and suggestions that are needed to the unconscious mind. Even though this technique will need a bit of experience and training to do, it is an efficient and powerful approach to use. The factor that it works so well is because it can get rid of the resistance and clog that the subject may have to the recommendations.

Two main kinds of metaphors will often be used in this type of hypnosis; isomorphic and interspersal. For the metaphor that is interspersal in nature, the command that is described has been embedded into the story and would not be easily discovered by the subject exterior of their unconscious mind. The other type, isomorphic metaphor, is a bit more familiar and provides instructions to the unconscious mind just by presenting a story to the subject that will offer an ethical at the end. The unconscious mind will be able to draw a one to one relationship connecting the aspects that originate from the story and the elements that feature the behavior or issue scenario.

An example of an isomorphic metaphor is the story "Boy Who Cried, Wolf." Numerous moms and dads will use this story to teach their children about lying, mainly if their kid tells a lot of lies. After hearing the story, the unconscious mind of the subject would see a parallel between the informing of lies and the young boy who is in the story. They would see that telling lies might lead to the kid, and a disaster might be more going to stop depending on the procedure to avoid that catastrophe from happening.

Embedded Technique

Another type of hypnosis is called the ingrained method. Throughout this procedure, the hypnotherapist will inform the subject of a fascinating story. This story is suggested to help distract and engage the mindful mind of the subject. It will also contain indirect ideas that are concealed within the story but which will be accepted into the unconscious mind of the subject. Through this story, the therapist will use procedure directions to direct the unconscious mind of the subject to discover the memory that is needed. This memory is generally about the learning experience that is suitable from the past. The hypnotist will then be able to use that discovering experience to help them to make changes to their present.

Nero-Linguistic Programming

With Neuro-Linguistic Programming or NLP, hypnotherapists have an excellent selection of the techniques that they can use in the hypnosis process. When using the process of NLP, the hypnotherapist will have the ability to use the very same thought patterns that are producing the problem in the subject. This can save alot of time compared to going through the procedure of recommendation. The idea patterns that are used with stress or excessive appetite will be used to help remove the issue that the subject is dealing with. If used with a licensed hypnotherapist or psychologist, NLP can be very useful. There are several kinds of NLP programs that have been used by hypnotherapists. Some of the most commonly pre-owned types of NLP include NLP Anchoring, NLP Flash, and NLP Reframe. NLP Anchoring. The very first kind of NLP that will be talked about is NLP Anchoring. An excellent way to consider how anchoring works is thinking of an old tune that you know. Have you ever sat in a car and truck and heard a tune that you have not heard in a long period? Did that song trigger some sort of sensation in you that came from the past? The very first time you listened to that song, or at some point down the road when you heard it, you were going through these feelings, and the unconscious mind attached these feelings to that particular song. Through this process, the song would become the anchor for these feelings. Now, each time that you hear this specific song, you will trigger the brain to have these feelings all over again. This is an excellent example of anchoring.

Many hypnotherapists have found that anchoring is a beneficial technique for them to use in hypnotizing their subjects. For instance, if you have a memory of being rewarded for doing something right in the past, the therapist will be able to enter into that specific memory and help you to recreate the sensations that you were going through at the time. The therapist will tell you to make some moves, such as; touching two fingers throughout the entertainment procedure. Now each time that you contact your fingers together, you will be able to feel those same happy sensations again.

The process of anchoring can operate to encourage you to achieve something by associating pleasant sensations with it. This technique is mostly used to help individuals find the inspiration they require to stick to losing weight and keeping a diet. The hypnotist will work with the based on produce a positive anchor that is related to the mental image of the subject-- in this case, it will be the subject thinking of themselves in a thin and attractive body. When the subject images this image again, they will activate the anchor and get the favorable inspiration that they need.

There is a significant boost in the motivation for weight reduction in those who undergo hypnosis compared to those who do not. The process of anchoring can be used in a range of different circumstances to help in the self-improvement of the people.

NLP Flash

NLP Flash is another kind of hypnosis that is thought about to be incredibly powerful and done by a certified specialist. It is usually used to change thoughts and sensations around in the unconscious mind of the subject. It can be a great way to help those who feel chronic stress or are addicted to a substance. In this procedure, the rapist will change the feel of the subject around, instead of a particular act bringing enjoyment, that act will begin to bring discomfort, or somewhat of a specific action bringing stress, it will bring the subject relaxation. Somebody who is addicted to a compound, such as cigarettes or alcohol, will find a feeling of pleasure and happiness when they consume that substance.

Through the technique of NLP flash, these sensations will get changed around, leading to the subject sensation pain or discomfort when they take in the content. This can help them in overcoming their addiction more effectively.

Those who are going through a great deal of tension have likewise discovered the technique of NLP Flash to work well for them. When a person is feeling chronic stress, they may have difficulties in controlling their high blood pressure and their tempers and are going to feel uncomfortable a great deal of the time. Given that stress is so hard on the body, there are numerous clients happy to go through the NLP Flash hypnosis to assist them in relaxing. With this strategy, the subject will discover their triggers of tension and redirect them so that those triggers begin to launch sensations of relaxation in their minds instead.

This method has been shown to be efficient in snuffing out the conditioned actions in the mind of the subject. An example of this is smoking cigarettes. If you are a cigarette smoker that delights in a cigarette while having a cup of coffee in the early morning, your unconscious brain is going to start matching these two habits together. This suggests that the subject will get a craving to have a cigarette anytime they take pleasure in a cup of coffee, particularly in the early morning. When the subject goes through the NLP Flash method, they will discover how to dissociate the two occasions from each other. This enables the cigarette smoker to have a cup of coffee without also getting the desire to smoke at the same time. When attempting, this makes it an even more effective technique to use to stop smoking.

NLP Reframe

The 3rd form of NLP that has been used in hypnosis is known as NLP Reframe. This strategy is powerful because it works so well in helping the subject to change how they behave. To this process, the hypnotist needs to understand there is a secondary gain or a positive outcome. That is achieved by each of the habits that a person performs. The result that happens from the behavior is significant since that is the reason the subject is acting in the very first place. Regardless of the importance of the result, the behaviour adopted to accomplish the outcome is not that crucial.

During the process of reframing, the hypnotherapist works for working out and reason with the unconscious mind of the subject. The goal is to get it to take control of the duty for making the subject replacement in some brand-new behavior that is effective and available at achieving the needed secondary gain. While this is going in the mind, the brand-new behavior will be acceptable to the subject in their conscious mind. For example, if the individual remains in the practice of eating when they are sad to make themselves feel better, the hypnotist is going to perform this technique to teach the unconscious to do some other activity. The act of consuming may be replaced with a workout or checking out a good book, helping the subject to drop weight, eat healthier, and feel much better all around.

Video Hypnosis

While the other kinds of hypnosis have been trendy in assisting subjects in getting rid of challenges and change how they think to live much better lives, brand-new hypnosis types are continually being established.

Among the most recent kinds of hypnotherapy that have been developed is video hypnosis. This kind is used through business methods so that individuals can purchase them and use them at their leisure. The techniques used in a few brands of video hypnosis are also based upon the Neuro-Linguistic Programming innovation discussed earlier. This implies that the video hypnosis method will work based upon using the existing idea procedures that the subject has instead of using hypnotic suggestions like standard techniques.

The reason video hypnosis has increased is that more than 70% of individuals have found that they discover things more comfortably and more quickly when they see things compared to when they just hear the info. The subject's mind will find out to change the feelings that it is having along with its visual associations automatically on the mindful level while enjoying the visual motion pictures that are provided.

While there are several types of video hypnosis programs that are readily available, **Neuro-VISION** is one of the most popular since it has been established using a few of the very best methods in the industry. This kind of video method works to train the unconscious mind of the subject through digital optics, which is a high tech simulation process on the computer. This will free the subject of their tensions, prompts, and obsessions.

Through this procedure, the smoker will discover that stopping smoking is easy, the dieter will lose their hunger, and those who feel tension will begin to relax more. It will typically take a minimum of a few sessions of video hypnosis to see outcomes, although some find that merely one seeing will start to show some of the issues that they want.

Subliminal Hypnosis

The final type of hypnosis that will be talked about in this chapter is subliminal hypnosis. Typically the subliminal hypnosis messages will be put on a recording for the subject to listen. The record will have two tracks, and each one will speak with a different part of the mind. One path will consist of a cover sound that will be heard through the conscious mind of the subject. The cover sound is typically straightforward for the brain to listen to, such as nature sounds or music. The other track will consist of the right ideas that will be heard through the unconscious mind of the subject. These suggestions present on the second track will be repeated over and over throughout the entire session.

Subliminal programs can be dipped into any time and in any location. You could be listening to these messages while you are working or even while watching TV. The most beautiful part is you will not need to stop the job that you are doing and take a seat and relax like what is required with NLP or standard hypnosis. Sometimes, subliminal programs will be included in your routine hypnotic programs.

Using subliminal programming is not that common. The majority of people will pass by this approach to change their routines and behaviors. Research has revealed that subliminal programs are not that useful; therefore, they will not have the ability to replace NLP or hypnosis. By some accounts, it might take more than 80 hours of listening to the subliminal message before it has an impact and numerous times even that will not suffice for many people. According to Joel Weinberger, a teacher at the Adelphi University and a psychologist, regular audio subliminal tapes that can be bought at stores or online simply do not work.

Subliminal psychodynamics might work as long as there is some kind of visuals present. The popular options offered only contain acoustic elements. The auditory is inadequate to make this approach deal with its' own. The subliminal idea will require to be combined with other kinds of hypnotherapy to have the efficiency that is desired.

Despite the representation of hypnosis by the media, it is not a wicked plot that is meant to take control of the minds of reluctant subjects. If the subject is not ready to go through hypnosis, it is quite much impossible to get them to go into the transformed state. Frequently, the use of hypnosis is to help others improve their lives.

This could be in the form of weight management, stopping smoking, improving other health conditions, and helping with persistent pain management. Each of the techniques is likewise crucial in assisting the subject in getting to their total objective. While all of them can be efficient, the expert that you choose to work with, as well as the concern at hand, will be used to figure out which of these approaches will best fit your requirements and assist in enhancing your life.

CHAPTER FIVE

Persuasion

Persuasion is another form of mind control that is in line with manipulation in that it works to affect the behaviors, motivation, intentions, mindsets, and beliefs of the subject. There are several reasons that persuasion might be used in everyday life, and often it is a needed form of communication to get individuals of different ideas on the same page.

In business, the procedure of persuasion will be used to change a person's mindset towards some product, idea, or event that is going on. Throughout the process, either composed or spoken words will be used to communicate thinking, feelings, or information to the other individual.

Another time that persuasion can be used is to satisfy an individual gain. This would include trial advocacy, when providing a sales pitch, or during an election campaign. While none are thought about as evil or wicked, they are still used in a way to affect the listener to think or act in a particular way. One analysis of persuasion is that it uses one's personal or positional resources to change the attitudes or behaviors of others. Several types of persuasion are understood; the procedure of changing the beliefs or mindsets through persuasion because of a motion to routines or feelings is recognized as heuristic persuasion, to reason, and logic is known as systematic persuasion; the process where beliefs and mindsets are altered.

Persuasion is a type of mind control that is used in society all of the time. When you speak to someone about politics, you may try to convince them to think the same way that you do. When you are listening to a political campaign, you are being encouraged to vote in a particular way. There is a lot of persuasions going on when somebody is making an effort to offer you a new product. This type of mind control is so common that many people do not even realize that it is striking them at all. When someone takes the time to convince you into believing perfects and worths that do not match up to your system of values, the issue will happen.

Various types of persuasion are readily available. Not all of them have evil intent, but all of them are going to work to get the subject to alter their minds about something. When a political candidate comes on tv, they are trying to get the subject, or the citizen, to vote a certain way on the ballot on election day.

The business advertisement is attempting when you see an industrial on tv or online to get the subject to buy that product. All these are types of persuasion that are bent at trying to get the subject to alter the method that they believe.

CHAPTER SIX

Deception

Lastly, deceptiveness is likewise considered a type of mind control because of the result that it can have on the subject. Deception is used to propagate in the subject, beliefs in circumstances, and things that simply are not true, whether they are total lies or just partial lies.

Deception can include plenty of various things consisting of sleight of propaganda, dissimulation, and hand, concealment, camouflage, distraction. Because the subject frequently does not know that any mind control is going on at all, this kind of mind control is so harmful. When they have been persuaded that one thing is real, the complete opposite is. When the deceit is concealing details that could keep the subject safe, this can get harmful.

Frequently, deceptiveness is seen during relationships and will generally cause sensations of mistrust and betrayal between the two partners. When deception happens, there has been a violation of the relational guidelines and can make it challenging for the partner to trust the other for an extended period. It can be especially destructive because the majority of people are using to trusting those around them, particularly relational partners and buddies, and expect them to be genuine to them for the most part. When they learn that someone they are close to is tricking them, they may have issues with relying on others and will not have the sense of security that they are used to.

Deception can trigger a lot of concerns in a relationship or within the agent and subject. Once they find out about the deceptiveness, the subject will have a lot of worries trusting the representative in the future. When the deception is done to help out the relationship, there will be times. When someone states something to suggest about them, these would consist of things such as not telling a spouse. Other times the deceptiveness is more harmful or spiteful such as when the representative is concealing essential information from the subject or is even deceiving in the individual that they are. No matter what kind of deception is being deployed, many people concur that deceptiveness is harmful and ought not to be done.

CHAPTER SEVEN

Body Language Codes

The Secret Question Code

How will you know what others are thinking about, how will you know what they are trying to find, and what will offer you a clear picture of the roadway, which you will follow in the persuasion procedure?

There is an answer to each question, and this rule is a principle; you call it (A response for each issue).

Regrettably, some salesmen are characterized by exceptional sales ability to speak, and you find them throughout meetings, talking, and talking without stopping, presenting more and more details. Sometimes they succeed and very frequently, they stop working. Yes, everybody thinks that the sales guy has to speak without disturbance, but this is entirely incorrect. You talk, and the client listens, you come out from the conference without the smallest idea in your mind of what the customer wanted.

Technique #1 (The Question): This Strategy supplies extensive research on the depth of the mind of the other party for a clear photo of the way of approaching to persuade this person. How do you get this picture? Yes, it holds, through a question. For that reason, it is merely asking the question as many as you can. Here is how to implement this method. From now on, you will begin any discussion with anyone else with questions. Do not talk about yourself; simply start by asking questions consistently. We will discuss what you will be asking about. Let us assume you want to persuade someone of your product, and you just have 10 minutes. If you are a normal male, you will start immediately to discuss your product, and you will duplicate a lot of times about how much fantastic and efficient is this product is, and so on. The possibility that the customer will purchase this item has to do with 50%.

If you are an expert in the science of persuasion, as you will become later, you will spend the first 6 minutes listening to your customer after each concern you asked. Then you will discuss your product based on his responses for 2 minutes. You will sign the contract and take the cash and provide him with the item in the last two minutes. The success rate is 90%.

In any discussion from now on, we will divide time into areas: 60% of the time will be committed to get to understand much better the other party through using several strategies, including concerns. We will find out in particular when, where to enter, how to end, and from where to come out. We will draw a map of the other individual, to collect information about him/her, and to understand how to operate? 30% of the time will be for persuasion, and the last 10% will be to close the discussion. Let us know more about this technique: Questions used by the persuasion expert include:

1. Determine the worths and primary requirements

2. Determine the direction of the conversation

3. Understanding the internal system for decision-making

4. Knowing rejection elements and clarification.

"People do not understand what they think in and do not know why they believe this!"

Therefore, we use concerns to clarify the values, beliefs, and views to comprehend the other party and manage the discussion better. Did you understand that it is impossible to ask a concern without getting an answer to it? Even if the other individual does not talk, he will answer it with his mind and his body language. Now I'll leave you with this discussion that occurred to me in among the conferences. Think deeply, and diligently with creativity, and I desire you to concentrate on the way the questions and how I could handle to talk and look for the golden piece of information, the secret to encouraging this customer to buy my item:

Client: Let me think about it!

I: Of course, you need to think of the subject; however, what avoids you from making a choice now, is it the power of the business that I represent?

Client: No, of course, I am confident that your company is one of the most influential businesses in this location; however, I require some time to believe!

I: So, it is our service that you do not like?

Client: Of course I like it, this is an excellent service, and we need it, I told you I require a long time to think about all the possibility

(Notice here how I make the client reveal that he desires the service, and it is a fantastic - Adherence to the concept Law)

I: Are we talking here about the regular monthly payments and costs?

Client: *Yes, in reality, I think I need to consider how I can manage these payments*

I: How much precisely do you anticipate that you will be able to pay in one month?

Client: *I believe we will have the ability to provide over $ 800 a month*

I: Gorgeous, however, you require this service, and as I stated, you need it now, (he did not say that - inject the memory with false information)

Client: *Yes, we require it, but the payments.*

I: So, we are discussing $ 860 a month. Do you think that your requirement for this service will make you save $ 30 a day to get this service?

Client: *Haha, I do not believe that this is hard for sure!*

I: What do you think about signing the order now, so I can schedule the service for you today when I return to the workplace so you can be able to get it tomorrow!

Have you seen what happened? If I were not a specialist of persuasion or having the wisdom to understand questions, and how to use them I'd wouldn't have changed the course of any discussion; I will not have the ability to change the customer's decision from allowing me to think of it (and 80% this means that he will not purchase) to (I do not believe that this is undoubtedly challenging). I asked about the reason for the rejection and a question after another until I got the result where I can resolve it and succeed in signing a contract.

Therefore, the questions manage the conversation and lead to the manner you have to take. However, there are some cases whereby impractical question get you to the outcome when the other party is connected emotionally to his opinion.

For example, you talk to a lady in one of the cafés and to convince her that you are a nice person. She has to drink a cup of coffee with you. Rationally, she is convinced but declines your request because she is emotionally connected with somebody else. You talk with somebody to sell your luxurious and stunning car, and he refuses to purchase it because this person wishes to have Porsche and absolutely nothing else. Logically, you will get him to the point that your car is the best option for him, but he is associated emotionally with something else. Sometimes you can change the point of view of someone;

however, for the most part, you will not have the ability to reach a satisfying result for both parties. Therefore, you need to ask and then ask over again until you are familiar with the other party very well; to know how he believes, behaves and responds, what he desires, and what he cherished. Throughout the following codes, we will give many examples consisting of drawing the road map to the other party through questions; however, I choose to mention them promptly.

COMMUNICATION STYLES CODE

How do other people talk? What does it mean? How do they speak, or how do they behave? This does not matter to others, but, as a professional in persuasion. You have to know who the other person is.

As you know, it is much easier to put people in appropriate boxes, groups. In truth, it is difficult because everyone is different from each other in personalities and communication designs. But we share some of the qualities that, as a specialist in persuasion, I can figure out the portion of which 70% of who the other person is, sometimes it can reach up to 100%, and possibly down to 1% at different times. But what concerns me is that I won't know who is sitting before me in a meeting or a service lunch. It may take years to develop a connection and relationship. I will only need essential headings to know which group that person is, so I can determine the proper interaction design to get approval.

Of course, as I stated, it is difficult to give a test of character for each person you want to know how to talk to. However, we'll know a little; the essentials which will enable us to develop our discussion techniques to match others.

According to Psychology Experts, Human beings characters are divided into four primary types:

- Leader
- Analytical
- Friendly

Everyone falls in one of these groups. Many have a leadership personality. Others are friends, and many may have a bit of this and that. However, no one is beyond these groups. Before you learn more about the qualities of each of these four groups, we need to understand that there is nobody who is a leader, or only an expert, preferably one may have a mix of all attributes in various degrees and percentages. All we need to do is to have a short conversation with this person before we start speaking about what we wish to do to encourage him/her. We have to know which of these groups has a higher percentage forming his/her character; this code is intriguing! Because you'll see yourself first, where you are, who you are, you will discover your friends, your employer at work, you will see where your husband is, and after that, we will learn how to convince everybody about these groups.

The Leader, the main qualities of this person are:

- Does not lose time

- Desires the results at any expense

- Constantly in charge

- When he/she is accountable for the work, it encouraged that the work ends with positive and satisfying results

- Always positive of himself! / herself

- Independent in his/her way of thinking

- Likes obstacles

- Decides quickly and right away

- Anticipates everyone to deal with all his or her capabilities

- They are considered to be in one of the most antagonist group compared to the rest groups

- Develops his/her world around him/her and takes pleasure in being in control

- Desire everyone to know his/her achievements

- Thinks quickly

- Makes the decision based on the information available to him/her now

- Is successful in any job as long as he/she is in charge

- Expect everyone to be on time and pay attention to those who do not

- You will find him/her in a position like Chairman of the Board of Directors, a supervisor of the company, or a group supervisor.

How to persuade a leader?

Here is the method:

In truth, a leader is the most convenient kind of person to persuade, but you need to give him the details in a different order to get the best result:

- Considering that the leader takes decisions quickly and immediately based on the information available to him/her, your speech needs to be quick and include only vital information
- You need to be ready to talk fast
- You need to hit the subject right to the point without introductions
- You need to tell him/her what the product you offer does, or what is the idea that you are passing across to him/her. Do this quickly
- Stay away entirely from information, as he/she does not require them. Remember that he/she can be making decisions based on the information available to him/her
- Because he/she has no time to waste, so you need to be brief in what you are discussing

- He/she is trying to get results, so you have to tell him/her what will happen if he/she uses your product now; what are the benefits that he/she will derive from your product/service?
- You continuously have to stop talking by providing him/her two options to pick one of them," Would you like to have a meeting on Sunday or next Thursday?"

For that reason, these are the bottom lines through which you need to engineer and design your speaking to persuade a leader. Now, imagine you have to meet a business owner or a chairperson of a board of directors of a big company, to set a date for a meeting next week. This person is on his way out of his office, approaching his car, and you have less than a minute to get his/her approval. Bring out a paper and make a note of 5 to 6 sentences just to persuade him/her that he should meet you, as he needs what you sell. When you finish writing these sentences, bring your mobile phone, start the stop-watch, and begin talking as if you are talking to that individual, look at the stopwatch, you have just one minute! Do you find yourself persuading?

The Main Analytical Features

- Always thinks rationally

- Searches for logic in everything he/she sees

- Slow in making decisions

- Prepares continuously before he/she speaks

- Tries to achieve excellence

- Excellent at numbers, analysis, operations

- Derives a pleasure in solving issues

- Likes to talk in-depth about the problems

- Delight in working alone in any function designated to him/her

- Always follows the directions and regulations provided to him/her

- Life does not have a lot of experiences, and is closer to the routine

- Quick on his/her consultations

How to convince an Analytical Person

- The analytical person does not decide instantly! He/she needs a lot of details, proof, numbers, and always logical.

- He/she needs a lot of time to make a decision, so you have to give him/her the opportunity and time to think
- Be prepared to get in the minute details
- Deliberating with an analytical individual can be extended to more than an hour
- You have to take care to speak the unclear language of a sales individual that does not suggest a lot to him/her
- You have to show to him/her how much you will reduce the expenses if you state that the item decreases the costs
- You ought not to put pressure on him/her to make a choice now, however, on the contrary, offer him/her the opportunity of (Sir, Madam, I believe you need a long time to think of this, this is my number, at any time)

Do you know anybody around you who has this personality? Try to think of him/her now. I do not know, however whenever I consider this character, an image comes across my mind of somebody wearing a striped t-shirt, wearing glasses, his hair does not follow any hairdo, but it is neat. He/she is walking more slowly than others, and you will always see him viewing television all through the night, viewing the news, paying electrical energy and water bills, and he is still on time. What about you?

The Sociable Main attributes

- Takes pleasure in social relations

- Likes to be around with others

- Loves to enjoy things and to be fascinating to others

- Loves enjoyable

- Tends to amplification and the generalization in his/her speeches

- Speaker and lives the moment

- Bad at managing the details

- Relocations in every direction

- Promotes long times on the phone

- Acts through his sensations

- The best in public relations, reception, and customer care

- Sometimes, you find him/her as a company manager or a group leader; however, he/she is not as good as the lead person because his/her decision-are made based on his/ her feelings and not through logic.

How to encourage a Sociable

Here is the method:

- Encouraging a friendly individual is easy; however, he/she takes time
- He/she does not care excessively about time in any case
- He/she needs to know that what you offer will be approved by his/her group or his/her friends
- He/she needs you to concentrate on the value of what you give and the effect on his/her social image
- You have to give him/her examples of other individuals like him/her using what you used, or doing what he would do
- Because he/she will feel bored right away, do not squander his/her time in detail
- You need to focus more on fun feelings that he/she will feel if he/she is going to use your product, concept, or your deal. Let him/her think and picture it. You will discover him/her more likely to imagine than other groups

- Concentrate on words like (enjoyable, pleasant, intriguing, Hamas, Exciting) and plug it in, including direct exposure
- Do not give him time to believe because it does not know the worth of time, so put him in a state of beautiful feelings and linking what you want to get and then ask him to give you a decision immediately.

Now think of the picture of this person, link it to one whom you understand that possesses such qualities, contact him now, and request to give him a cup of coffee this evening. Prepare any idea you want; any sense, and you will attempt to persuade him today using the method above, simple! Isn't it? Now assuming you are calling him, and convince him over the phone. I want you to encourage this friendly person, who will say that he is busy tonight, to go out with you. Prepare what you would say now through the points listed above. Call consistently.

The Friendly Main attributes

- Steadfast in his/her feelings
- Rational

- Everybody likes him/her for his/her good morals and his/her friendly relationship with everybody
- Peaceful and likes remaining in a relationship
- Performing through his feelings as a friendly person
- Doesn't hurt the feelings of others and does not think that others might harm his/her feelings
- He/she is real in his feelings and believes what others need to say about their feelings
- He/she likes to remain in the status quo, and dislikes change
- He/she is a beautiful listener; he/she concur with others even if he/she is not encouraged about what they have to say
- Everybody is looking for his/her aid and suggestions at difficult times and issues to talk to him/her
- He/she never takes danger in any choice
- He/she find it difficult to say either "yes" or "no" to you
- He/she does not like arguing and discussions
- He/she is the slowest in deciding
- He/she is the most devoted amongst all groups.

How to persuade the Friendly

Here is the technique:

- Based on the essential attributes above, it is clear that this individual is the hardest to be convinced
- Frankly speaking, the entire procedure is enjoyable and makes you feel that you are tired and deserve success when you finally convince a person of this Group
- Speaking with him excitingly or in details, will get rid of the whole process immediately, so avoid it
- Because he/she will respect that and will accept your relationship quickly, you have to develop a relationship with him in the beginning (and this is not tough!
- You have to make him/her feel that he/she is making the best decision
- You have to say to him/her repeatedly, "You have taken the best decision" at least five to ten times, and not in a precise, direct method
- He/she needs to feel that you are a friend to accept you
- You can persuade him easily through embarrassment, as he realizes it difficult to decline demands from others; however, in this case, you'll get (one yes), and after that,

you will lose him/her permanently. For that reason, do not use this method

- Other, then, in one case, when you ask him/her over the phone, for instance, to satisfy harder, here it is OKAY to embarrass him/her and repeat the demand until he/she agrees. Because when you please him/her, you will initially develop a relationship before you start revealing what you want him/her to concur on.

Which one are you? Are you a leader or analytical? Do you keep in mind the number of your conferences with others, and where mistakes happened? For instance, before you learn this? I used to consider myself a leader and an analytical picture; how did I know? Now, I kept in mind a few of the conferences and talks with a friendly person; but, I did not know how to do it. Can you think of how the discussion used to go on? I desired him/her to make a choice immediately, I used to overemphasize with logic and information, and it was as if I was giving him/her orders to make a decision rather than asking him/her politely. Can you picture why I did not get (yes)? Now I want you to keep in mind some discussions with your friends, your moms, dads, and your spouse, were you talking with them using their approaches or using your design? Do you see the difference now?

Most of the info will occupy your mind, and you are talking with others aiming to place them in one of the groups. For that reason, you have to follow the way I think it is useful and necessary and does not lose time as well; the percentage is indeed only 10% to be the best group. However, it will minimize the possibilities from four to two or three, which will put you on the best track. Then you will find more by doing it several times! We have to reduce the possibilities from the beginning. When I please somebody, I do not know the groups he/she is; I ask him/her to make a decision that has nothing to do with what I am going to say to him/her later.

What would you like to drink (we are in a café)?

His/her answer:

1. What do you think? (Sociable or friendly)
2. I feel that I desire orange juice (choice based on feelings; Friendly or Unfriendly)
3. Coffee is the best option in this list, and after that, closes the menu while he tossed a quick look (leader)

4. Coffee is the best option - check out the majority of the menu (more analytical)

5. He/she does not look at the menu at all and already chooses (leader)

6. He/she takes a great deal of time (analytical-friendly)

7. I do not know; I have not tried pineapple juice here in the past; I hesitate that is bad so that is what I want to have, as in the previous time, Turkish coffee (analytical or friendly)

Hence 10% here, 5% there will lower the possibilities for you. Include what we have actually found from body language and what we can learn later about methods and signals, you will discover that you reduce the possibilities to 90% and will get the appropriate response. You need to keep an eye out for something; everyone has little of this and that, so you need to know where and when he/she is in this group or that! You need to start now, mixing methods with this person. For instance, you wish to convince me now by sending me a message on the website or e-mail to give you a special session in the secret codes free utterly for you!! You need to integrate between handling the leader and friend. You need to increase my interest in doing it, you must not waste my time, you need to press me to make a decision, however with caution, and you need to do it logically. Now, write me a message, use these methods, convince me to give you a private course in the secret codes free of charge just for you, and send it to me when you are ready.

CHAPTER EIGHT

Setting Boundary Not To Be Manipulated

By now, you must have the ability to know the value of setting limits for both personal and relationship growth. Many people will have a hard time establishing and maintain boundaries because of some misconceptions. Because they are scared of the repercussions, such borders can have on their values and their lifestyle.

For instance, some individuals hesitate about losing all their friends when their limits appear to be too high and unrealistic. It is essential to handle common boundary myths and accept reality to set limits effectively.

Misconception # 1: I may look self-centered if I set boundaries.

This misconception or objection is frequently raised by people who believe or feared being considered as self-centered or self-indulgent when they set boundaries. Many people are scared of being accused of doing not have issues for others when they set borders. Hence they offer upsetting such limits. In reality, setting boundaries does not make you self-centered, setting limits will help you take care of others, while you safeguard yourself from being at the receiving end of every misgiving. Individuals who set boundaries the most are typically the most caring ones in the world because they have discovered that through borders, their requirements have been taken care of; for this reason, they have lots of energy and time to take care of the needs of others.

All our needs, desires, and selfishness only consider our desires, whereas borders think about our needs. When we concentrate on our desires, we might lose focus and balance, and somewhat of pursuing our healthy goals through setting limits, selfishness might force us to work to please others. Trying to satisfy our needs does not make such requirements bad.

Misconception # 2: Boundaries are symptoms of disobedience and un-submissiveness.

Many people are scared that setting boundaries or limits will signal to their partners, co-workers, friends, or bosses that they are disobedient and rebellious. Some people think that saying "No" to something good just implies they are unresponsive. Thus they take part in every social event or take whatever that is thrown at them. Doing everything that comes, your doing has no spiritual or psychological worth. When you do things out of inner voice, however, your heart is not in it, then you are wasting your time and trying to please others. Focus on setting borders in whatever you do so that you don't do too much.

Outwardly need something when we mean No merely makes you a liar. If we state No to great things only because of our self-centered desires, then such a limit makes you disobedient.

Misconception # 3: Setting limits indicates I am always upset.

For many novices who are just setting borders, they may realize that they suddenly begin to tell the truth and take responsibility for all their actions. These people may feel that some type of "anger cloud is surrounding them," many especially when they become conscious where their limits are being violated. When you start setting boundaries, you might fear that you can be offended easily, and this might get you confused. This is simply one of the essential things you may experience at the beginning of setting limit; however, you will overcome it, when individuals start to understand what you stand for. Borders do not cause anger in us; however, if you see the limit set as the source of your passion, then you misunderstand your emotions. Your emotions must be the signals that need to tell you about something-- for instance, Your fear ought to advise you to move away from a dangerous situation, while anger needs to ask you to challenge an imminent risk.

You ought to remember that a mad circumstance is a warning that you are in imminent danger of being attacked or injured. For this reason, anger ought to be viewed as a positive indication that you will be manipulated, or your boundary will be violated. While your worry might tell you to withdraw from a situation, anger will help you advance and protect your fence. There is no reason to be scared when your boundaries are being breached; instead, the violence should help you not to bea violent, however affordable way to inform the violator to stop breaking your borders.

Don't simply let your anger out; instead, you need to discover to protect whatever is yours more properly without showing unfavorable feelings.

Misconception # 4: When I begin creating borders, I might be injured by others.

When you set limits with people who do not regard constraints, it is frequently complicated. Indeed, many people don't like it when we present our arguments and viewpoints, and may snap at us or simply withdraw from connecting with us. However, this does not mean you need to treat people gently always because they don't appreciate your border. You should not refrain from reality, because those who enjoy the truth will quickly want to associate with you. It is essential to be liked by people who understand the fact than to be disliked by many who wish to oppress and take advantage of you.

Ask yourself the question; what if the person who hates you for your borders is your spouse? Will you then abide by no boundary guidelines just to maintain peace in your relationship? Or will you just endure his wrong sides and let him breach your borders and still abandon you. If you hesitate to the survival of your relationship and keep allowing your partner to maltreat you, then you might not have the guts to set the boundaries. It is ideal to discover the hidden character of your partner and solve all fundamental problems instead of preventing the problem.

It is highly likely that you will get hurt from setting borders; however, your relationship will likely end up being deeper.

Misconception # 5: When I set limits I might injure others.

You may end up frustrating other people occasionally when you set boundaries, particularly when you value the happiness of such people. Some of the cases where you might hurt people when you set limits to, consists of:

- When a friend desires to borrow your car when you need it

- People might call you for a social gathering preparation, which is when you are physically down, or

- When a relative enters into a difficult financial situation; however, you can't loan him the specific quantity because you have some monetary responsibilities to care also.

Depending on how you see boundaries, you might harm or might not injure others. However, nothing can be much better than knowing the truth, and the truth is that setting borders around your treasures are the only way you can safeguard them from being taken, ruined, or trampled with. When you set boundaries for the wrong function or motive, then you might hurt the ideal people. Still, you need to remember that saying No for the best reason will not cause injury to other people, although it might trigger discomfort, and they need to look elsewhere for the same favor.

It is not your responsibility to meet the requirements of everyone, though you must do everything possible to help others achieve their goals (however not at the hindrance of your happiness). You should help others quickly when you have the resources to do so, and even when somebody dares to have a problem. You might have other more significant issues to compete with, for this reason, you need to try to fix the most critical problems in your own life before thinking about meeting the needs of others. Sometimes you might be the one who gets declined; hence, you need to develop some supportive relationships where you do not enslave yourself because of others.

Misconception # 6: Boundaries might become difficult to accept.

Some people hesitate to establish boundaries because of the bad experiences they had in the past regarding previous borders that were set for them. Obtaining to accept the limits set by others can be unpleasant. Given that nobody likes to be declined, you need to prepare your mind for unfavorable answers you get when you cross the boundaries set by others. You may ask yourself, why is it difficult for people to accept bounds?

- During your youth, you may have been hurt by certain unsuitable limits set by people. When parents set borders around their kids, for example, the kids might feel some sense of not being wanted, and this may follow them through their adult years, and often feel unaccepted when the word "No" is said to them. The bright side is that old problems don't have to stick in your memory correctly when you discover to accept other people's limits.

- Individuals who were gravely injured by borders in their youth typically attempt to leave from the harmed by satisfying the same bounds against others. Setting boundaries on other people can not allow you to impost hatred on them because they will just move away from you for the best reason. Never predict your old feelings from the boundaries set for you, for your kids, good friends, colleagues, and other people around you.

- The inability to accept limits set by others, specifically in your marital life, might tend to do with your objectives of unfaithful to your partner.

If your emotional satisfaction will always depend on your spouse's being on your side at all times, then something is not right about the relationship because you are the only one who set borders.

- Failure to accept boundaries may show somebody has problems in taking responsibilities. Often, many people are accustomed to counting on people to save them from problems they deliberately induced themselves. These people believe the duties of their wellbeing remain in the hands of others; for this reason, they feel dejected when their recipients do not satisfy such requirements. When you learn to take responsibility for your own life, you will be positive about setting limits.

Misconception # 7: Boundaries may result in feelings of guilt.

This is another misconception many people can't comprehend, the factor being that the sense of responsibility may become an obstacle for them in setting borders that can be advantageous. It is difficult to say No to somebody who has helped us in the past, particularly with money, efforts, and time. All you need to do is show thankfulness for what has done for you, instead of setting boundaries. Many are not comfortable with taking gifts because we always think sometimes we need to pay in return. And some people do not wish to accept presents any longer because they do not want to fret about repaying in the future.

Some people do not give selflessly; however, they give for future purposes. You can discriminate between these people by the way they respond after you thank them for their gesture-Kind givers don't also wait on you to thank them because they need nothing from you. If the giver is outraged by doing you a favor, then the person sees the present as a financial investment. If your appreciation is enough, then he or she probably wants absolutely nothing in return.

The concern of thankfulness and borders should be kept different because limits must not be nullified sense of appreciation; thus, this misconception holds no weight.

Misconception # 8: Boundaries will separate me from others.

Lots of people are scared of setting up personal limits since they are scared of ending up being social outcasts or appearing different from others. These individuals tend to prevent anything that may make them look different from everybody. You need to know that opting for the crowd always will rob you of your uniqueness, even if it will make things different from you.

You need to know that you have a free-will and duty for yourself and those delegated in your care. Thus you should set boundaries to secure everything treasurable to you. You must decide the options you want for your life, and you don't need to end up being a puppet for somebody to run to you. Your relationship with the crowd should have a limit; thus, your boundaries should be totally under your control. When you see that your property line will be appreciated, then you can re-adjust your borders (for example, make it less complicated).

When they see how in a different way you do things, edges will make you different, and individuals will eventually learn to separate and respect you.

Misconception # 9: Boundaries will end up being permanent and may produce a long-term gap between me and others.

Do not be deceived; there is absolutely nothing like a long-term limit, and the reason being that circumstances change; hence you have to change. Lots of people believe that once boundaries are set, they can never be removed; they think that limits will create a permanent space between them, their friends, household, and associates. You must learn to adjust your borders to present truths and scenarios; hence you would not look like a problematic person.

Boundaries are not developed to get rid of closeness; instead, they produce more powerful bonds and more duties.

Limits will cause character maturity and also help build the type of nearness we should have as human beings. Naturally, immature people will want to stay away from us when we create boundaries, but they return to their senses when they see the real significance of why you set such borders.

All the limit misunderstandings highlighted above ought to be considered simply mistaken beliefs, practical limits will assist you in representing yourself and saying No to reckless activities.

Personal Boundary-Common troubles you might deal with

Borders, mainly when an individual can offer the flexibility and development that you want. Establishing boundaries is difficult, similarly complying with such limits is even more challenging. You need to remember that the function of setting limits is to safeguard yourself from bad influences. There are quite a variety of ways of explaining the problems of establishing and abiding by boundaries; these are:

- Compliance with borders may merely mean saying "Yes" in the red things. This also means that the limit setter may stop working on setting the limits and might continue to feel guilty of being controlled by others.

- Avoidance of restrictions may simply mean one is saying No to the Good. The avoidant of a limit might choose to close the gate of their love and affection to others.

- Failing to stay under control merely indicates one stops working from acknowledging the "No" of others. The controller, in this case, will attempt as much as possible to break the borders set by others through manipulative and aggressive means.

- Unresponsiveness to limits simply means the failure of the unresponsive individual to like others. Unresponsive individuals will naturally fail to hear about the needs and desires of others; for this reason, they fail to offer responsibility to care and help.

You don't need to abide by everything thrown at you; if you do, you will wind up carrying the concerns of others. Nevertheless, controllers, on the other hand, want others to bring their problems. Avoidants will typically want to shoulder their own worries since they do not look like they need help from people. The non-responsive people will naturally refuse to assist others even when the concerns of others' are ending up being unbearable.

There are four major problems connected with personal limits, and some people may establish issues in a lot of these locations at the same time.

Limit problems are:

- Compliance

- Avoidance

- Other-control

- Unresponsiveness.

Compliance a significant issue in the border setting

Compliance is the primary and most prominent issues dealt with by people outside a border set for them. The agreement is frequently the hardest problem of limit that can be taken. Compliance in the edge is difficult to say No to others. We reside in a conflicting world, and if we do not learn to say words like "I disagree," "It injures," and "That is wrong," we may find it challenging to make it through this evil world. Lots of females are trained to be loyal and submissive, and by doing such, they think they are inferior to males. Those who comply with boundaries typically give-in to the demands of others in other to prevent disputes, and that can require them to be subjected to controlling and manipulative people. It is not ideal for taking any violent situation. When you are not submissive, then you may influence the other person to change from his or her ways and welcome the fact.

Compliance as an issue in boundary-setting might take place for several reasons, and these consist of:

- The fear of hurting the feelings of other people

- Fear of losing a friendship or being abandoned

- Fear of getting punishment for other people's anger

- Fear of being labelled as "Selfish"

- Feeling of guilt.

Being over-critical about one's assessment can require one to participate in self-condemning acts, and many people's consciences are so weak that they end up being quickly manipulated. Complaints are merely unstable; hence you can't depend on them to decide for a very long time.

Avoidance: an issue of border setting

The limit setting will assist keep the evil out of reach and also allow us to welcome the good. Some people seem to have problems with this think since they have set their limits as walls because they enable the boundaries to be secured where nothing is allowed; this means nobody can reach out to them for good, and this might be a disaster.

Avoidant individuals who set limits intentionally scare people who desire to reach out to them and take care of them. People who struggle with avoidance problems in border settings will continuously wish to avoid individuals so that they would not discover their needs. Avoidants deeply desire somebody to come to their rescue, but the wall they made around themselves is too strong. Some people may also say that their problems can not be compared to what others are facing; thus, they wish to fix their issues by themselves.

Lots of males often strive to ignore their emotional requirements because they want to preserve a self-dependent sharp image to people; they declare whatever wanted or needed, whereas they are empty inside. Males don't want to be viewed as weak. Some people who attempt to avoid conflicts are constantly drained pipes in their regret of allowing others to use them for their selfish purpose; for this reason, they continuously lose energy with nothing to change it.

Control: a problem in border setting

Setting boundaries can be hard and complicated; however, this can end up being more comfortable when people appreciate such limits. Some people always want to be in control of others, and when we state No, they simply view it as an obstacle to change our minds-for circumstances, sales, and market males and females will always desire to convince others to purchase their items. Controllers will always have issues respecting the limits set by others. Controllers will try to use many ways to get others to shoulder their loads, and they can be found in two forms:

- Aggressive controllers

- Manipulative controllers

Aggressive controllers are the most bothersome people around because they do not care about other people's borders. They just want the whole world to be on their sides once they make up their mind. They continuously want the final say, and they simply overlook their duty and rely on others to handle them. Religious fanatics are good examples of aggressive controllers who do not appreciate limits set by others, but they want to enforce their own beliefs and ideas on others.

Sometimes, we can just enjoy the qualities of some aggressive controllers, especially when they put such conditions to significant use.

Manipulative controllers are sensible to a particular extent in recognizing the boundaries set by others. Manipulative controllers will attempt to do everything possible to persuade others to quit their limits for them to reject their desire to control others even though it is fundamental that their last resort is to get the attention and control of others for their selfish interests.

The majority of controllers often end up isolated, but that doesn't mean they don't get to have people around them; however, they are uncertain whether individuals around them remain because of worry or dependence. If you are a controller who wants to manipulate others, then you need to face your fear by offering up your control over others. Otherwise, you might end up losing regard, and your boundary may be violated when you violate other people's limits.

Complaints and avoidants might also be controllers at the same time, but they clearly say what their limits are.

An unresponsiveness: an issue in the border setting

Unresponsiveness explains a mindset where some people live their lives without surrounding the well-being of people around them.

Unresponsive individuals believe that life is complicated, and everybody needs to manage his or her personal service.

Unresponsive people typically look like if they are not distracted by things happening around them, as long as they accomplish whatever they want. While unresponsiveness might flourish when setting boundaries in the business world, a lack of sensitivity in a marital relationship is a different case. Because it makes other partners look cold, and such may result in the breakup of the relationship.

Unresponsive individuals will naturally shrug off the requirements of others when they make known such conditions, and for unresponsive people, requirements are simply diversions and nothing more.

Unresponsive people think they are not accountable for how others live their lives, and they do not feel the necessity to be connected to the people around them or perhaps help them carry part of their responsibilities.

Unresponsiveness in boundary-setting may become even more complicated when people involved are also delighting in aggressive or manipulative control behavior.

People that are unresponsive and controlling at the same time never see beyond themselves. However, these people often find it incredibly tough to get out of their issues because there might be no one to come around to assist them due to their separated lifestyles.

In-completeness usually is the most striking feature of people who experience unresponsive behaviour correctly when setting their boundaries; they may look happy with what they have when they are empty (a lack of happiness within).

It is necessary to start dealing with problems connected with limit setting whenever they begin to show up. This will help in identifying areas where you will need help, and you wouldn't end up isolating yourself simply because you have built a wall around yourself. The more boundary you set, the more problems you might face, thus it is an excellent idea to keep limits to a manageable number at a time so that you can quickly determine violators and re-adjust realistically. In this case, you might need some routineevaluation of the performance or effect of the boundaries you set.

CPSIA information can be obtained
at www.ICGtesting.com
Printed in the USA
BVHW081330181120
593625BV00013B/1394

9 781801 200295